The Complete Guide to

Boykin Spaniels

Jordan Honeycutt

LP Media Inc. Publishing
Text copyright © 2024 by LP Media Inc.

Publication Data

Jordan Honeycutt
The Complete Guide to Boykin Spaniels – First edition.
Summary: "Successfully raising a Boykin Spaniel from puppy to old age"
Provided by publisher.
ISBN: 978-1-961846-06-7
[1.The Complete Guide to Boykin Spaniels – Non-Fiction] I. Title.

Main Cover Photo – Courtesy of Tyler Coleman
Cover Photo Top Left – Courtesy of Jovaane McDonald
Cover Photo Top Middle – Courtesy of Shelby Wagenseil, Photo by Liz Atterbury
Cover Photo Top Right – Courtesy of Austin Boyd

Design by Sorin Rădulescu
First paperback edition, 2024

TABLE OF CONTENTS

Chapter 3

Preparing for Your Boykin Spaniel...................25

Chapter 4

Bringing Home Your Boykin Spaniel 39

Chapter 5

Chapter 6

Chapter 7

Chapter 8

Chapter 9

Chapter 10

Chapter 11

Hunting and Fieldwork

Chapter 12

Chapter 13

CHAPTER 1

Breed History

Humble Origins and the History of the Boykin Spaniel

> *Boykin Spaniels are a relatively young breed of dogs. They have only been recognized as a breed by the AKC since 2009. If you are looking for a hunting or hunt test prospect, pedigree increases the odds in your favor. Proven pedigrees from dogs that have titles across multiple venues show that they can do the work. I like to tell people Michael Jordan's son has a much better chance of being good at basketball than mine. It doesn't guarantee that it will happen, but the odds are in his favor.*
>
> JONATHON GRABARA
> *Tradewater Kennels*

The Boykin Spaniel is a relatively new breed, created in the early 20th century in a small town called Boykin in South Carolina. The breed has humble beginnings that began with a small, stray spaniel-type dog. It is said that a banker named Alexander White found the small brown spaniel outside a church in Spartanburg, South Carolina, and gave him the endearing name Dumpy.

When White took Dumpy hunting with his other retrievers, he was surprised to see that Dumpy showed instinctual hunting and pointing behaviors that matched White's purebred retrievers.

*Photo Courtesy of
Dawn and Bill Crites
Lily Pad Spaniels*

White decided to send Dumpy to his friend and hunting buddy, a man named Lemuel Whitaker "Whit" Boykin, for training. Training proved to be successful, and the little brown retriever became adept at retrieving and flushing. Dumpy was so successful that Whit Boykin decided to use this spunky stray as the foundation stock, combined with the Chesapeake Bay Retriever, Springer Spaniel, Cocker Spaniel, and American Water Spaniel, for the breed that would eventually be called the Boykin Spaniel.

According to the Boykin Spaniel Society (BSS) breed standard, the Boykin Spaniel was developed with a strong emphasis on its working abilities and practical functionality as a hunting dog. Size and weight were chosen to ensure the breed's ability to move effectively in tight spaces, such as small boats, while retaining the stamina and strength required for long hunting sessions. The breed was crafted with a focus on field performance—agile, small enough to be transported easily, and strong enough to retrieve game, making it ideal for South Carolina's diverse terrain and waters. The Boykin Spaniel, therefore, became affectionately known as "the little brown dog that doesn't rock the boat," reflecting both its hunting heritage and its utility for hunters.

While the breed stayed local to the area where it was created for years, Boykin was a resort hunting destination, and visitors began to take notice of the small spaniel and its tenacious spirit. Eventually, the breed spread to the rest of South Carolina and then across the East Coast.

DID YOU KNOW?
Boykin Spaniel Society (BSS)

The Boykin Spaniel Society (BSS) is an organization dedicated to preserving and promoting the Boykin Spaniel breed. Founded in 1977 by the Boykin family and a group of passionate enthusiasts, the BSS has played a pivotal role in maintaining the breed's hunting heritage. The primary goal of the BSS is to ensure the integrity, health, and working abilities of the Boykin Spaniel by upholding a breed standard that emphasizes the dog's versatility and temperament. In addition to these goals, the BSS provides extensive information and education about the breed and organizes various events, including hunting trials and specialty shows. For more information about the BSS, visit https://boykinspaniel.org/

The Differences Between AKC and BSS Standards

The Boykin Spaniel Society (BSS) and the American Kennel Club (AKC) have both played key roles in defining and promoting the Boykin Spaniel, though each organization has its own priorities that are reflected in their respective breed standards. Understanding these differences requires a look at the goals and history of each organization.

The Boykin Spaniel Society was founded in 1977 by the Boykin family to preserve the breed's hunting prowess and maintain its original traits as a versatile working dog. The BSS created its studbook in 1979, and closed it in 1980, ensuring that registered Boykin Spaniels came from a specific foundation of registered stock. BSS standards emphasize the working characteristics of the Boykin Spaniel—primarily focusing on qualities that make the breed an excellent hunting companion, such as stamina, size, and coat type suitable for fieldwork.

The AKC recognized the Boykin Spaniel much later, in 2009, with its standards placing an equal emphasis on the breed's appearance, temperament, and versatility, including both family and hunting suitability. The AKC standard tends to favor a more polished appearance, making it ideal for conformation showing while still acknowledging the breed's working abilities.

Photo Courtesy of Reagan McColl

Key Differences Between AKC and BSS Standards

- **Focus:** The AKC standard balances the Boykin's hunting capabilities with its suitability for the show ring and as a family pet. In contrast, the BSS standard emphasizes the breed's field performance, retaining characteristics that are ideal for hunting.

- **Physical Appearance:** Both standards have similar height requirements, but there are differences in how weight and proportions are addressed. The BSS standard tends to focus more on maintaining a size that supports agility in the field. Coat types are also more flexible under BSS standards, prioritizing practicality for field conditions.

- **Tail Docking:** Both the AKC and BSS accept docked tails, though the BSS takes a more utilitarian view, treating tail docking as necessary for safety in hunting situations. The AKC, while acknowledging this practice, also notes tail appearance and carriage for showing purposes.

- **Temperament:** The BSS standard strongly emphasizes hunting drive, ensuring that Boykin Spaniels bred under their guidelines have an intense focus on hunting instinct and stamina. The AKC, on the other hand, gives more weight to the Boykin's temperament as a family companion in addition to its hunting abilities.

These different focuses between the AKC and BSS reflect their broader goals: the BSS aims to preserve the hunting capabilities of the Boykin Spaniel, while the AKC strives to showcase the breed's versatility in both family and sporting environments. The collaboration and occasional differences between these organizations are a testament to the breed's diverse strengths as a dedicated working dog and a loving companion.

What Is a Boykin Spaniel?

> "
>
> *Once you fall in love with a Boykin Spaniel, you'll realize you've found a true companion and friend. I always joke to people that Boykins are actually half human. They have intense eyes that seem to read your thoughts, and when reprimanded, they will act like you've broken their heart. The best family for a Boykin is one that is prepared to devote time, love, and energy to fulfilling their constant need for attention and exercise.*
>
> **AUDRA BOYKIN**
> *Legacy Boykins*
> "

The Boykin Spaniel is a medium-sized spaniel well suited to family and hunting life. According to the AKC, "A medium-sized flushing and retrieving dog known for its rich bro wn coat, the Boykin Spaniel is avid, eager, merry, and trainable. This adaptable and attentive house dog, as well as tenacious bird dog, was once South Carolina's best-kept secret. Boykins are medium-sized spaniels, larger and rangier than Cockers but more compact than Springers. The breed's hallmark is a beautiful sol-id-brown coat. Colors range from a rich liver to a luscious chocolate. The large, feathery ears hang close to the cheeks, setting off an expression of soulful intelligence. Bred to work in the lakes and swamps of their native South Carolina, web-toed Boykins can swim like seals."

Photo Courtesy of Jovaane Mcdonald

Not only are these dogs bred for hunting, they have charming dispositions that make life at home with a Boykin Spaniel fun as well. These dogs are gentle and excellent with children, highly trainable, adaptable, and typically great with other pets. This breed is just as lovely inside as it is on the outside!

Physical Characteristics

As Boykin Spaniels were bred to hunt, their physical features were intended to lend themselves to ease in the field. For example, their size and build must be strong and hearty enough to do the work but small enough to easily fit on small boats. Their coat should be long and thick enough to protect the dogs from heavy cover but not so long and thick that it is cumbersome in the field.

Boykin Spaniels are slightly longer than they are tall and should stand between 14 and 18 inches from the ground to the top of the shoulder blade. Their proportional heads hold medium-sized eyes that range in color from amber to various shades of brown. Their ears are set even with or slightly above the eyes and hang flat against the face.

These hardworking dogs were bred to be compact and muscular for optimal field performance, and their physical characteristics reflect that.

Coat Type and Color

> *The Boykin Spaniel comes in a variety of coat textures. While the color of a Boykin is either dark chocolate or liver, the coat can be smooth, wavy, curly, or a combination. An owner needs to take a look at the parents to get an idea of the coat a dog might have. I have had litters where all three coat combinations were seen in the pups.*
>
> NANCY DICKSON
> *Sunstar Kennel*

Boykin Spaniels have a medium-length, single coat, but they can sometimes have a double coat. Known for their rich coat color, Boykin Spaniels possess a liver or chocolate-colored coat that can range in texture from flat to wavy to curly, with a possible white patch on the chest.

According to the AKC Breed Standard, "Boykin Spaniels are considered a 'wash and wear' dog, easily going from the field to the ring. The ears, chest, legs, and belly are equipped with light fringe or feathering. His coat may be trimmed, never shaved, to have a well-groomed appearance and to enhance the dog's natural lines."

Tail Docking

A Boykin Spaniel has its tail docked to a length of three to five inches at maturity. This usually happens just days after the puppy is born. Tail docking is functional for this breed and is done to keep the dog's wagging tail from making too much commotion in the field and to prevent common tail injuries while working.

Though docking is often a controversial topic, in the case of the Boykin, it is done for the safety of the dog.

Typical Breed Behavior

> "
>
> *Boykin Spaniels are best suited for an active family who likes to include their dog in their lifestyle. Boykins have a lot of energy and were bred to be retrievers for bird hunters. So, they enjoy running, retrieving, and being the life of the party, whether they have a duck or ball in their mouth. Hence, if someone wants a versatile dog for competing in dog sports, the Boykin is a great option!*
>
> ASHLEY COOPER
> *Silver Preferred Breeder*
> "

The Boykin Spaniel is a force to be reckoned with in the field but also a wonderful companion at home. The dog's easygoing temperament means it is great with kids and other pets and aims to please. It is agreeable and eager to obey while also being sturdy and gentle.

Boykins are working dogs and have high energy needs. They will need regular exercise in order to stay happy and satisfied. Bred to be companions in the field, this breed wants to fulfill its work duties alongside its human companions and will potentially suffer if not given the opportunity to use these skills in some way.

Hunting Instincts

As has already been discussed, the Boykin Spaniel was bred with the intention of creating a hunting dog. Just as Dumpy, the dog that began this breed, had a natural adeptness for flushing and fieldwork, the Boykin Spaniels of today are bred with that same instinctual hunting prowess.

The Boykin Spaniel is said to be a versatile hunter and can be found duck, pheasant, goose, or turkey hunting. It is a dog of endurance. It practices a hesitant flush, waiting to locate the bird before

Photo Courtesy of Austin Boyd

following through with an aggressive flush. Pointing is out of character for the Boykin and is not typically accepted among the breed. The Boykin Spaniel is also a very strong swimmer and should take to the water willingly.

Despite their strong hunting instincts, the Boykin Spaniel is considered friendly and generally non-threatening to other small animals or pets. Of course, each dog is unique, and caution should be used; this breed, when introduced early and often, is typically agreeable with smaller pets. More on this topic can be found in Chapter 3.

Is a Boykin Spaniel Right for You?

> *Boykins are incredibly affectionate, smart, and loyal. They have a strong desire to please their humans. They are an intelligent and active breed, so families should plan to spend lots of time with their puppy during the first year so they'll have a great companion for life. Boykins need both physical activity and intellectual stimulation. Multiple walks per day and retrieving sessions are great ways to satisfy their need for activity. Multiple short training sessions in obedience, house manners, walking manners, and retrieving should be factored into each day. It only takes about five minutes per training session, but consistency is necessary to achieve your goals of having a wonderful companion that is enjoyed by your family, your neighbors, and any visitors to your home.*
>
> TABBY LANGLEY
> *Tabby's Sweet Boykins*

The Boykin Spaniel is a breed with a purpose. If you are looking for a reliable hunting companion, this breed may be exactly what you're looking for. However, it is not cheap to care for and maintain a valuable hunting dog. As we will discuss in a later chapter, training for a hunting dog can be very pricy. Before purchasing a Boykin, be sure that you have calculated the cost and that it is something you can afford.

These dogs are loving companions, but they are also high-energy and want to work. If you plan to spend plenty of quality time with your Boykin Spaniel and can give him the care and exercise he needs, this breed may be right for you!

CHAPTER 2

Choosing Your Boykin Spaniel

> "
> *Boykins are very active dogs that are loving and loyal. I look for homes with acreage, hunting, and/or training homes. These homes are usually very good at keeping the dogs active and moving. They are great family dogs and good with children as well. When talking to families/homes, I want to know what their plan is to keep the dog physically active. I typically stay away from townhouse and apartment-style living situations.*
>
> SCOTTY DUNNAM
> *Bluff City Boykin Spaniels*
> "

Buying vs. Adopting

Once you have decided on a Boykin Spaniel, the first step in your search for the perfect dog is deciding whether to purchase a puppy from a breeder or adopt one from a rescue. If your plan is to use your Boykin Spaniel as a hunting dog, you may envision raising one from a puppy for ease of training and adaptability. If that is the case for you, finding a reputable breeder is likely the best move.

If your heart isn't set on a puppy, adopting a rescue Boykin Spaniel may be something you're interested in. Keep in mind, however, that adopting a dog is not always as simple as rescuing a dog in need. These dogs often have special medical or social needs and will require a unique owner to meet those needs.

If you can provide the patience and care it may take to adopt a rescue Boykin Spaniel, please do! The bond between a rescued dog and its owner can be just as strong as the bond you form with a new pup.

One benefit of adopting a Boykin Spaniel is having the opportunity to know its personality before you bring the dog home. You will likely know ahead of time if the dog is good with children or not, if it has any

Photo Courtesy of
Theresa Miller

behavioral or aggression issues, and what its level of energy may be. As long as you ask the right questions, there should be very few surprises when adopting a mature Boykin Spaniel.

> *I would say to go with a breeder if you want a puppy that is health tested and proven in the field. Find one that raises the puppies in their home so they see the personalities and expose their pups to birds and water. I would look for a rescue to get a Boykin that is a mystery. One to love on and care for. One that needs saving. It may have health issues or be advanced in age, but deep down they are all Boykins. No matter what they have been through, they are very loving, people-pleasing, super-smart dogs. A rescue would be ideal for someone not wanting to go through the puppy stage.*
>
> DIANE WEBER
> *Webers Boykin Spaniels*

The Differences between Animal Shelters and Rescue Organizations

In the United States, there are three classifications for pet and animal rescues: municipal shelters, no-kill shelters, and nonprofit rescues. In this section, we will outline the key differences between them.

> *There are two rescue organizations for Boykin Spaniels—Boykin Spaniel Rescue and Operation Little Brown Dog. Both do an amazing job rehoming Boykin Spaniels.*
>
> DAWN CRITES
> *Lily Pad Spaniels*

*Photo Courtesy of
Kelly Graham*

Municipal Shelters

Municipal shelters are funded and run by local governments. These shelters take in stray animals and animals abandoned or surrendered by their owners. Animals are given a limited amount of time to be adopted before they may be euthanized due to a lack of space for more incoming animals.

Municipal shelters house their animals in a kennel-like setting in one centralized location. Many have veterinarians on staff to provide basic care and sterilization. While most have a small paid staff to care for the animals, many facilities rely on volunteers to help attend to the animals and clean kennels. Adoption fees are usually lowest at municipal shelters, and nearly all require an animal to be spayed or neutered before leaving the shelter.

While shelters are an excellent way to find local pets in need, you likely won't find a purebred Boykin Spaniel in the shelter. However, you may find a mixed-breed dog that meets your qualifications. Municipal shelters are almost always fighting an overpopulation problem. Be aware that if you choose to adopt from a municipal shelter, it isn't uncommon for even a non-aggressive dog to act fearful or show aggression when in a stressful environment such as a shelter. This phenomenon is called "kennel syndrome," and it can sadly keep some good dogs from being adopted. Ask if your shelter allows a trial period where you can take the dog home for a few days to see if he is a good fit for your family. This will give you the opportunity to see his personality shine outside of the high-stress kennel environment.

Photo Courtesy of Becky Stanley Preston

No-Kill Shelters

A no-kill shelter will only accept as many animals as it can handle. These shelters will not euthanize a dog due to lack of space, but they will turn dogs away. Many dogs find themselves at a no-kill shelter for an extended period of time, months, and sometimes even years, before they are adopted.

Some no-kill shelters have a central location with kennels to house the animals, but many often utilize foster homes for animals as well. These homes allow the dogs to live a more normal life while they are waiting for their forever families. Sometimes, that is just what a dog with kennel syndrome needs to become more adoptable.

HISTORICAL FACT
Origins of the Little Brown Dog

Boykin Spaniels are an all-American breed originating in South Carolina in the 1920s. These little brown dogs are excellent hunting companions and beloved family dogs, bred for hunting waterfowl in the Wateree River swamps. Lemuel Whitaker "Whit" Boykin, a sportsman from South Carolina, is credited with establishing the breed that now bears his name. Reportedly, the predecessor to the modern Boykin Spaniel was a stray dog rescued by one of Whit's friends. Whit employed this stray, nicknamed "Dumpy," as a retriever, and later bred this dog to produce what is now the Boykin Spaniel.

Nonprofit Rescue

These organizations are typically operated by a crew of volunteers and are privately funded or dependent on donations. These organizations will utilize foster homes for their animals, and many have no centralized facility at all. Private rescue organizations are often breed-specific, meaning they are dedicated to rescuing one dog type, such as the Boykin Spaniel.

Because these nonprofit organizations typically do not have an on-staff veterinarian to care for the animals, they often must pay full price for services, which can become a significant expense. Due to these higher expenses, rescues typically have much higher adoption fees and adoption standards than shelters. Not only do many require a detailed application, but some also require a home inspection before an adoption is approved.

Much like purchasing from a breeder, these private rescue organizations will often maintain contact with the adopter for several months to ensure the placement is going well and may even do a follow-up home visit. Many also have policies in place mandating that a dog be returned to them if the adopter is no longer able to care for it for any reason.

Tips for Adoption

Many animals are homeless through no fault of their own. Unfortunate circumstances can find any dog in a situation without a loving place to go home to. Not all dogs in need of a home have special needs. Perhaps a family is forced to move and is unable to take the dog along, or a death leaves the dog without its owner or home. Dogs in these situations are often highly adoptable and will adjust easily to a new home.

If you do choose to adopt a rescue Boykin Spaniel rather than purchase from a breeder, reach out to all your local shelters and let them know what you are looking for. While chances are slim that you'll find a Boykin in a local shelter, it doesn't hurt to have them keep an eye out just in case.

Another good place to begin your rescue search is through a local breeder. Find a Boykin Spaniel breeder and ask them if they have any information on rescues. If not, take your search online. If you decide to rescue a dog in need, seek out a reputable organization quickly, as many breed-specific rescues have waiting lists for available dogs. Don't hesitate to get your application in if you see a dog you're interested in!

Breeder Reputation

If you choose to find a Boykin Spaniel from a breeder, it is crucial that you choose one with a good and upstanding reputation. With so many people flippantly breeding dogs from their homes these days, it can be challenging to know who to trust. There is a significant difference between a breeder who is breeding for the sole purpose of profit and one who is dedicated to the betterment of the breed.

Photo Courtesy of
Edith Hines
Woodland Holler Boykins

One significant difference between a responsible breeder and one who is not is that backyard breeders are rarely doing the testing required to ensure the health of their litters. Some even turn out to be puppy mills, places where dogs are kept alive to do little more than pump out litter after litter for profit. Often, dogs in puppy mills are kept in small cages in unclean conditions.

A reputable Boykin Spaniel breeder will be regarded as such among the Boykin community, so seek advice from those who own or enjoy the breed. If you find a reputable breeder without an available litter, ask for references to other respected breeders.

The breeder should be willing and proud to show pedigrees and get health testing done. They should show these papers without being asked. They should not say things like 'I didn't test the dogs because of the cost' or 'It's really not important.

JAMES ZILKA
Muddy Creek Boykins

Finding a Breeder

> To find a Boykin puppy (or older Boykin), the very best place to start is at BoykinSpaniel.org, which is the website for the Boykin Spaniel Society. On this page you will see a list of breeders that have agreed to comply with the recommendations of the society to produce healthy dogs. Any breeder on this list will have done all recommended DNA and OFA tests. Be careful when talking to breeders who say they've done testing but seem casual about it; you want to pick a breeder who truly loves the breed and cares about the longevity of the dog and the breed. Ask lots of questions. Do they breed other kinds of dogs? How long do they keep the puppy before pick up? Why did they choose these specific dogs to breed? What characteristics do they add to the gene pool? Above all, trust your gut, and if you get a bad feeling from someone trying to sell you a puppy, steer clear.
>
> AUDRA BOYKIN
> *Legacy Boykins*

It is both easier and also more challenging to find a reputable breeder with the help of the internet. While a quick search online may bring up a plethora of options, not all of these options will be good. There are several questions you need to ask to discern a good breeder from someone who is just trying to make a quick buck. They are as follows:

Q: Can I Visit the Breeding Facility?

A: The answer to this question should always be a resounding yes. A breeder might not allow you into certain areas of the facility for the safety of the puppies. There is a concern about tracking in diseases that could be detrimental to a young puppy's undeveloped immune system. However, a quality breeder should always allow you to come on-site and see other dogs in their program. If they refuse, this could be a sign they have something to hide, and you should reconsider.

Photo Courtesy of Michael Jamison

Q: How Long Have You Been Breeding Boykin Spaniels?

A: You should only buy from an experienced breeder who is well established, so the answer to this question should be several years. A quality breeder who has several years of experience will know all the ins and outs of breeding for only the most desirable traits and healthy dogs.

Q: Can I See the Veterinary Records for Both Parents?

A: When investing your time and money into a Boykin Spaniel puppy, you will want to have an open and transparent line of communication with your chosen breeder. If the breeder is not willing to share the medical records of the puppy's parents, this is a signal that you should find another breeder. Both the dam and the sire should have been checked by specialists and cleared for defects. The breeder should also provide proof of genetic testing.

Q: Do You Ever Sell to a Broker or Pet Shop?

A: If the answer is yes, walk away from this breeder immediately and do not support them. A responsible breeder, breeding for the betterment of the dog's health and appearance, will never sell one of their animals to a broker or a pet store. Reputable breeders want to meet the families of each of their puppies to be sure they will be properly cared for. Puppies found in a pet shop are bred for profit alone and come with no health guarantee.

Health Tests and Certifications

> The Boykin Spaniel Society is the registry that originated with the development of the dog. Their primary goal is the constant betterment of the breed. Currently they advocate that sires and dams be screened for seven known breed-specific conditions: pulmonic stenosis (heart), hip dysplasia, patellar luxation, eye anomalies, and DNA tests for collie eye anomaly (CEA), degenerative myelopathy (DM), and exercise-induced collapse (EIC). If these tests have not been done and mating is planned accordingly, then a multitude of issues can arise.
>
> MARK LEE
> *Holland Ridge Boykins*

As with any purebred dog, the Boykin Spaniel is prone to developing certain genetic conditions. Before agreeing to purchase a puppy, ask for a detailed list of the tests the breeder performed on the parents and ask for copies of the test results. These tests should be performed by certified specialists for each potential ailment, such as a board-certified veterinary cardiologist and ophthalmologist. Just because the breeder had the dogs checked out by a general veterinarian does not mean they were genetically tested for undesirable traits.

Breeder Contracts and Guarantees

When it comes to finding a breeder, look for one that guarantees the health of the puppies in the contract. Ideally, the breeder should be willing to refund most or all of the cost of the Boykin Spaniel puppy in the event any congenital health conditions appear within the first year. However, not all breeders may offer such a refund, so it's important to clarify the terms in advance and understand what kind of support will be provided if any health issues arise. Beware of breeders who only offer to replace the puppy with a healthy one, with no option to receive a refund instead. If the breeder produced a genetically unhealthy puppy the first time, why would you want to bring home another puppy from the same place? Many people are also unwilling to return their dog for a replacement, as they have already become attached. This is a low-risk guarantee from a breeder and may be a warning sign. On the other hand, a responsible breeder will always take back a dog that you can no longer care for, no matter the reason.

There are often stipulations in a breeder's health guarantee. These may include waiting to neuter or spay your puppy until after the one-year mark to ensure the joints are fully developed and that you are feeding your Boykin Spaniel a proper diet and taking it on regular visits to the vet. A responsible breeder will want their puppies to remain in perfect health; unfortunately, not all owners care for a dog the same, and health results will vary depending on lifestyle and diet.

Some breeders use a Limited Privilege (LP) registration policy, which requires that puppies meet specific health standards, such as passing the Boykin Spaniel Society (BSS) health panel, and in some cases, earning performance titles before being eligible to produce registered puppies. If you wish to breed your Boykin or compete in dog shows, you will need to ensure you meet these requirements and work with a breeder who offers full registration. For more details, you can refer to the BSS website.

Despite health guarantees and contracts, no breeder can completely guarantee the health of every single puppy that leaves their facility. If something does go wrong with your puppy, before putting the blame on the breeder, it is important to understand any role you may have unknowingly played in the situation.

Picking a Puppy

> *Choose the litter based on the sire and dam. Then let the breeder interview you and let them select the best pup from the litter that will suit your needs.*
>
> **BILL CRITES**
> *Boykin Spaniel Society Hunt Test Chairman*

Once you have found a reputable breeder to purchase a Boykin Spaniel from, you can begin looking forward to the day when you will be paired with your puppy. Although all Boykin Spaniels will share general traits within the breed standard, personalities will vary just as they do in humans.

In many cases, the breeder is the best choice to decide which puppy will be the best fit for you and your family. Their years of experience with the parents give them a unique insight and ability to predict how the traits of each littermate will develop. After getting to know your family, lifestyle, home, and plans for the dog, a good breeder will be able to recommend a puppy that they feel will best fit into your life and suit your needs. It's recommended that you trust this advice, as it's usually the right choice.

In cases where the breeder is not able to give their recommendation, then it will be on you to decide which puppy is the best fit for your family. This is often a guessing game, and many new owners base their selection on emotion, choosing the "cutest" or "most playful" puppy. However, a puppy may just look cute and helpless because it's shy and timid and would fit best in a quiet household. That "playful" puppy may be strong-willed and aggressive, making training more of a challenge.

When you can, rely on the breeder to pair you with the puppy that they feel best fits your needs.

Raising Multiple Puppies from the Same Litter

Most breeders highly discourage purchasing two puppies from the same litter, and for good reason. Raising a single puppy is a challenge, but raising two is especially challenging. Not only are you doubling the work of raising a puppy, but each puppy will need independent, one-on-one training and attention, meaning you will be investing a great deal of time into your dogs individually until they are well-trained.

In addition to the extra workload of raising two puppies, the bond formed between littermates is strong and may interfere with the bond you are hoping to form with each puppy. If you wish to have an unbreakable bond with your dog, it is wise to only bring home one at a time so that those deep bonds can form. A reputable breeder should always advise against getting two dogs at once, and many breeders will refuse to sell multiples unless you have proof that you can care for them both properly.

If you wish to have two or more Boykin Spaniels, purchase them at different times so that you can establish a relationship with each puppy before introducing another. Even then, when bringing home a second puppy, keep him separate from your other dog for a time so you are able to establish that human-to-dog bond with him as well. Even still, no matter how hard you try, you may find that your two dogs pair up and develop a bond that potentially surpasses the bonds between you and each dog.

CHAPTER 3

Preparing for Your Boykin Spaniel

> **"**
>
> *Boykin Spaniels love people and want to please them. They are very easily trained. Also, they like treats and respond to positive training. Be careful—their intelligence might surpass their owner's. Owners may find themselves being trained by their Boykins. One-word commands are best. Make sure the whole family is using the same commands for the dog.*
>
> ROSLIN COPELAND & GINGER HURLEY
> *Texas Trace Boykins*
>
> **"**

Take the time to prepare your home for your new Boykin Spaniel before pick-up day to make the transition easier for you and him. From preparing your family members and other pets to purchasing supplies and preparing a space, this chapter will walk you through all you need to know about preparing for your Boykin Spaniel.

Preparing Children and Other Pets

Whether you have children or fur-children, you need to prepare everyone in the house ahead of the arrival of your new addition. Bringing a puppy home can be exciting, but it can also be stressful for other members of the family. Be patient as all settle into a new normal and a new routine.

> **❝**
>
> *On the bell curve of being curious and active, Boykin puppies are toward the top! Some people say it is the hunting drive bred into them for generations that propels that activity. Like human babies, Boykin puppies explore their world with their mouths, and that can get them into trouble. An unorganized, untidy home with children's socks and hair scrunchies on the floor is a recipe for disaster. The family needs to be educated to use the hamper and keep the environment free of temptations while the puppy is small. Develop good family tidiness habits before your new puppy arrives.*
>
> PATRICIA DOWNEY
> *Bayhill Boykins*
>
> **❞**

Because most children are typically excited to bring home a new puppy, adjusting them to the idea will likely be easy. The most important aspect of preparing your children is teaching them how to safely handle and care for the pup. A small child can unintentionally harm a young Boykin Spaniel simply by trying to show affection in a manner that is a little too rough. Also, puppy teeth are sharp, and your small pup can unintentionally hurt your child by trying to play. Because of this, you should carefully supervise interactions between children and the puppy.

Adjusting current pets can be a bit more challenging. Depending on your current pet's personality, transitioning a new puppy into the family may be easy, or it may take some work. Either way, begin warming your current pets up before puppy pick-up day so they aren't overwhelmed by the new "intruder."

A great way to start integrating your new puppy into your home is to start introducing his scent before he even arrives. Talk to your chosen breeder and ask if you may take home a toy or a blanket with his scent before pick-up day. Be sure to ask ahead of time, as they may ask you to provide them with the toy or blanket. Once you have an item with the dog's scent, put it in the common area of your home for all existing pets to encounter for several days before your Boykin Spaniel arrives.

When the big day finally arrives, and it's time for your new pup to come home, be very cautious with the first introductions. If possible,

Photo Courtesy of Kristen Booker

have someone help you so that there is an extra set of hands around in case you need them. Always begin introductions in a neutral area where your current dogs are less likely to become territorial. However, for safety reasons, this neutral area should not be a public park or anywhere else other dogs frequent because this may put your unvaccinated pup at risk. Instead, choose an unused area of the yard around your home or the home of a friend or family member.

Keep the first meeting brief so that no one is overwhelmed. All dogs should be leashed with a bit of slack so they can safely greet the new addition. After seeing first reactions, use your judgment and slowly give them more freedom to get acquainted as you see fit. Remember, stop all interactions and separate the dogs before any parties become overwhelmed or stressed.

If the interactions between your existing dogs and your new puppy aren't going as well as you'd hoped, you may need to take more extreme, slow measures. If this is the case, try keeping your dogs in separate rooms but close enough that they can smell and hear each other. Make sure you do not keep your current dogs out of a space they usually have, as this may cause jealousy issues. Again, use your judgment and allow the dogs more freedom with each other as you see progress. It may take a great deal of patience, but usually, dogs will become acclimated to each other and form a bond.

If you are introducing your new puppy to a resident cat, keep both your cat and puppy safe by maintaining control of your puppy or by allowing them to meet while one animal is contained in a crate or separated by another barrier. Allow them short, controlled interactions at quiet moments of the day until they are both calm around each other. Always make sure your cat has a safe place to retreat to, preferably off the ground, such as a cat tower. Never force your cat to interact with your new puppy.

While a new dog is exciting, it can unintentionally become the focal point of life for a while. After all, puppies are much like babies! Remember to show your other dogs and pets some extra attention and love so they know that they are still important members of the family and will not be forgotten. This can go a long way in helping everyone acclimate to the new addition with a good attitude.

Puppy-Proofing Your Home

> 66
>
> *Small toys, socks, underwear, rubber bands, paper clips, etc., are all things that should be placed out of reach of a Boykin puppy. They are curious and will eat or chew anything! Puppy proof as though you have a toddler mixed with a small velociraptor entering your home.*
>
> **EDITH HINES**
> *Woodland Holler Boykins*
>
> 99

Just like we must baby-proof our homes for curious little humans, puppy-proofing your home before your Boykin Spaniel arrives is an essential task. Although he may look harmless and innocent, that little shark-toothed puppy will likely find himself in mischief at one point or another, so it's important that you give him a safe area to explore. There are many seemingly harmless things in a home that can pose a danger to a young Boykin Spaniel.

HELPFUL TIP
Full Grown Boykin

Boykin Spaniels have a medium-sized muscular build and are slightly longer than they are tall. Adult male Boykins typically weigh between 30 and 45 pounds (13.6 to 20 kg), while females weigh slightly less, ranging from 25 to 35 pounds (11 to 16 kg).

Tuck Away or Remove Electrical Cords Within the Puppy's Reach.

Even the most docile puppy may be enticed by the allure of an electrical cord. It is imperative you remove all cords from his reach to protect him from this hazard. If you cannot remove the cords from your puppy's reach, you may want to invest in some cord protectors. These cord wraps usually come infused with bitter flavors to help deter your Boykin Spaniel from chewing. If you find you have a particularly stubborn chewer, you can spritz the cords with hot pepper spray.

Invest in Fully Enclosed Trash Cans if You Do Not Have Them Already.

Do this for the kitchen, bathroom, and office trash cans. While the paper in your office trash can may not pose much danger, it will be a mess after it's been shredded by puppy teeth!

Lock Away all Drugs, Chemicals, and Cleaning Supplies.

If you tend to keep any medications in an area that your puppy may be able to reach, be sure to move those to a higher location, such as a dedicated, locked medicine cabinet. Puppies explore with their mouths, and snatching a bottle or box of medication off the sofa table could prove to be fatal for your new puppy.

Also, move any chemicals, cleaning supplies, dish pods, or laundry detergents into an enclosed area out of reach of your puppy. This includes any rat bait or poisons that your new puppy may find enticing. Even if these items are in an area of the house where your puppy will not be allowed, it only takes one curious adventure for your new pup to encounter something that could be harmful to him.

Remove Poisonous Houseplants.

If you don't already have pets in the house, you may not be aware that many houseplants are actually poisonous to dogs. Even some of the most common plants can be dangerous for a curious nibbling puppy. Some of the most common houseplants that are potentially dangerous for your new puppy are the corn plant, sago palm, aloe, and jade plant. There are many more common household plants that are poisonous to your dog. To find a complete list, visit the ASPCA website.

Don't worry; if you have one of the plants on this list, you don't have to give it up. Find a place that you are certain is out of reach for your puppy, and leave it there. Houseplants are a wonderful addition to the home and provide health benefits for you and your puppy. As long as you are aware of the dangers and plan accordingly, your pup should remain safe.

Beware of Xylitol.

Xylitol is considered a sugar alcohol and is commonly found in items throughout almost every household. As people become more aware of the dangers of added sugars, companies are turning to xylitol, an additive that tastes sweet but does not spike blood sugar and insulin levels like sugar. Xylitol can be found in almost anything, but it is commonly found in chewing gum, mints, candies, toothpaste, and even peanut butter. Xylitol is highly toxic to dogs and can cause dangerously low blood sugar levels, resulting in weakness, seizures, trembling, or even death. When dogs consume very high levels of xylitol, it may cause necrosis of the liver, which often leads to death.

Be sure to keep all purses and bags, which may contain gum, candies, or toothpaste, out of reach of your puppy at all times. Have a designated area for guests' bags so that they are not accidentally left within reach. Also, check all food labels for xylitol. Peanut butter is often recommended to give a dog medication, but some brands contain xylitol, so be sure to check the label first.

Keep the Batteries Away.

While you probably don't have random batteries lying around on the floor, you may have remotes or small electronic toys. If your puppy can get hold of a battery-operated remote or toy, he can chew it to expose the battery. Small-button cell batteries are the most dangerous, as they are small enough for your puppy to swallow. Swallowing a battery is a serious, life-threatening issue and can cause internal burns. Call the nearest emergency vet immediately if you suspect your puppy may have swallowed a battery.

Put Away any Children's Toys.

Children's toys are often made up of small pieces that are a choking hazard for your dog. Be especially careful with toys that contain magnets inside, as these pose an extra risk of internal damage when more than one is consumed.

Keep Toilets Closed.

Many people use automatically refreshing toilet bowl cleaners attached to the bowl of their toilet. These can pose risks to a thirsty pup. Remove chemical cleaners from your toilet bowl, or make sure you always keep the lid down.

Set Up Puppy Gates.

After you have puppy-proofed your entire house, designate a safe common area of the house for your puppy to stay. Use puppy gates to block any doorways or staircases so that it will be easier for you to keep a close eye on your new Boykin Spaniel. Having already puppy-proofed the entire house, you can be sure that even if your dog makes a great escape into a room where he is not allowed, the dangerous items have all been removed.

Accidents happen frequently because it only takes a second for a bored puppy to get into mischief. Preparation ahead of time is the key to avoiding these incidents and keeping your Boykin Spaniel safe.

Dangerous Things Your Dog Might Eat

> *Avoid toys that are easily destroyed, chewed apart, or which break into pieces. Chewing is a natural instinct in a pup, so avoid leaving shoes, socks, personal items, and valuables out where a pup can snatch them. Ingested items can become a costly vet bill.*
>
> NANCY DICKSON
> *Sunstar Kennel*

It can be tempting to share a bite of your own meal when those big, brown Boykin Spaniel eyes are looking up at you, begging for a taste. Though sharing table food isn't recommended, every now and then, you may want to bend the rules a little bit. When you do, it's important that you know exactly what your pup can and cannot have. There are several foods that, though harmless to humans, can cause illness or toxicity in dogs.

Chocolate – It is well-known that chocolate can cause major issues for dogs. Chocolate contains methylxanthine, a stimulant that can stop a dog's metabolic process. Methylxanthines are found in especially high amounts in pure dark chocolate and baker's chocolate. Too much methylxanthine causes seizures and irregular heart function, which can lead to death.

Xylitol – As discussed above, xylitol is particularly dangerous to dogs as it does not take much to cause a dangerous or deadly reaction. Vomiting is typically the initial symptom of xylitol poisoning. If you suspect there is a chance your dog has ingested even a small amount of xylitol, call the veterinarian immediately because time is critical.

Raw or Cooked Bones – Raw or cooked bones are a choking hazard for your dog. The bones can break or splinter and become lodged in, or worse, puncture the digestive tract. This is especially true with cooked bones of any kind, as they become dry and brittle. Pork and poultry

Photo Courtesy of Thad Frazier

bones are especially dangerous as they are more likely to splinter and cause issues.

Though controversial, some veterinarians say that raw bones of the right variety can provide healthy nutrients and help prevent tartar and plaque buildup in the mouth. These bones are recommended only under very close supervision and only for a few minutes at a time, keeping the bone in the refrigerator for a maximum of four days before discarding. If the bone is breaking or if your dog seems to be swallowing any pieces, discard the bone immediately. If you prefer to skip the risk, look for bones in the pet store that are meant to withstand heavy chewing.

Other foods that may cause gastrointestinal upset or injury to your dog are grapes and raisins; certain nuts, including macadamia nuts; avocados, apple cores, and seeds; and anything in the allium family, including onions and garlic. This is not a comprehensive list, so it is best to check with your veterinarian before giving anything from your plate to your dog.

Supplies to Buy Ahead of Time

After you have prepared your family and your home, it's time to purchase supplies! This can be a fun shopping trip for you, but it can also quickly become overwhelming. With so many cool gadgets and toys, it can be hard to know what you need and what is optional. This list of essentials will help you prepare for your pup and help your first few days together go smoothly.

Food and Water Bowls – Any walk down the food and water bowl aisle in a pet store can leave you confused and overwhelmed by all the options. There are different shapes, colors, sizes, and even materials. Some are ceramic, some metal, and some plastic. While it may be overwhelming, there are a few things to keep in mind to help you make the right decision for your Boykin Spaniel.

While plastic bowls typically come in lots of fun colors and shapes, they are lightweight, easy to tip over and move around, and are easily damaged by a chewing puppy. These bowls can also harbor bacteria in the scratches that are difficult to get clean.

Ceramic bowls can also come in fun colors and designs and are more difficult to knock over and spill. However, these bowls are breakable, so if your dog does knock one over, it is likely to break or chip. You can mitigate some tipping damage by placing your bowls on a mat.

Stainless steel bowls are both easy to clean and unbreakable, and they are an excellent choice. Some even come with a rubber or silicone base to prevent sliding and spilling.

Another option you will find in a pet store is an elevated bowl set. These are bowls that are set up off the floor so that your dog does not have to bend over as far to eat. These were created to help prevent the serious issue of bloat in some breeds, but studies have shown that elevated feeders can potentially contribute to bloat. Most experts say an elevated feeder is unnecessary and potentially problematic. If you are adopting a dog that has neck or mobility issues, then an elevated dog feeder would be something to discuss with your veterinarian as an option.

Many people also love the convenience of a self-filling water bowl. These bowls have upright jugs of water that funnel into the bowl as the water level is lowered. These can be a great option if you wish to avoid frequently filling the water bowl.

No matter which option you choose, make sure the bowls you purchase are large enough for your Boykin Spaniel when he is fully grown, or you will likely be buying another set as he grows.

Collar, Identification, and Leash – One of the first things you should do when bringing your new puppy home is to fit him with a collar. For safety, avoid attaching tags to the collar while your puppy is still young, as they can become caught on objects and pose a risk of injury. Instead, consider attaching a brass identification plate directly to the collar. For

identification, it's best not to include your dog's name, as this could make it easier for someone to manipulate your pet. Instead, you could include a message like "I am a Boykin Spaniel" along with your phone number. It's also important to have your puppy microchipped to provide permanent identification in case he ever gets loose.

Food – It's important not to abruptly switch your puppy's food when you bring him home, as this can cause digestive upset. Make sure you bring home enough of his current food from the breeder to last a few days, or get the name of the food so you can buy some. If you wish to switch foods, do it gradually over a few days. Regardless, make sure you have your puppy's food planned ahead of time so that you are prepared when he gets hungry!

Toys – Puppies come with lots of energy and razor-sharp teeth. This means if you aren't prepared to give them something to chew on, they will find something around the house to chew on instead. Have a minimum of four or five toys of different varieties to give your puppy so he has plenty of options to keep his attention. You may find that certain types of toys don't last long before being ripped to shreds, or you may find that your Boykin Spaniel loves to care for and carry them with him wherever he goes.

Grooming Brushes – Boykin Spaniels require regular grooming to keep their coats healthy and free from mats. Though, generally, puppies require less grooming than adults, it is crucial they become accustomed to the brush early on so that there is no anxiety about it later in life. Begin brushing your young Boykin Spaniel often with a small medium-bristle brush. Additional information on grooming will be provided in Chapter 13.

Puppy Training Treats – It is helpful to have a bag of treats to help with potty training and teaching basic commands in the early days. Look for soft treats that are healthy and natural. Be sure that they contain no animal by-products, and contain no artificial flavors, colors, or preservatives.

Crate and Pad – The crate is a safe place for your Boykin Spaniel puppy to be while you are away or when you cannot watch him closely. Though some dislike the idea of crates, they are an important and even imperative part of training when used properly.

NOTE:

While the crate provides a safe space for your Boykin Spaniel puppy, be cautious with using a pad inside the crate. If the puppy tends to chew, the pad can become a hazard if swallowed, leading to potential gastrointestinal issues. For new owners, it might feel harsh not to use a pad, but it is safer to avoid one initially if chewing is a concern. Crate training can still be comfortable without a pad, prioritizing safety as your puppy learns appropriate crate behavior.

Gate or Playpen – Having a safe area to keep your Boykin Spaniel puppy while he plays is extremely helpful. A gate blocking the doorway is an excellent and affordable option. A playpen may be a little pricier, but it is also a great way to keep your puppy safe from harm and your belongings safe from those puppy teeth!

Preparing a Space for Your Boykin Spaniel

We've already discussed the importance of puppy-proofing your space for your dog's safety, but what might that look like practically day-to-day? In this section, we'll go into detail about how to design a puppy-safe play place in a common area of your home so you can keep an eye on your sweet pup without being relegated to puppy duty all day.

Preparing an Indoor Space

Choose a space in your home where you spend the most time and create a safe area for your new puppy to hang out. This is where the puppy playpen or the door gates will become imperative. At the bare minimum, use a baby gate to block off hallways and other rooms where your young Boykin Spaniel may venture out of your sight.

Photo Courtesy of Janice Sears

Even better, set up a playpen in the middle of the room, away from furniture and other hazards like electrical cords, and fill it with dog toys. The "safe" area needs to be large enough for your Boykin Spaniel to play contentedly for a while but not so large he can still get into puppy mischief.

Remember, this is a temporary arrangement while your dog is young and in training. As your puppy matures, you will likely be able to expand his freedom little by little until, eventually, he has earned full rein of the house.

Preparing an Outdoor Space

For a breed that loves the outdoors as much as the Boykin Spaniel does, an outdoor space is a necessity. Without a proper and safe outdoor space, your Boykin Spaniel will likely feel cooped up and may possibly become destructive as a result.

When preparing your outdoor space, make it as puppy-friendly as your indoor space. Start by removing all chemical products from the area, including the garage. This includes any weedkillers, pesticides, antifreeze, or similar products. If you must keep them, store these items well out of reach on a high shelf, and push them back from the edges to prevent access, as some adult Boykins can counter surf when on their hind legs. Additionally, it's important to train your Boykin Spaniel that accessing elevated surfaces is not acceptable.

Fencing is also an important aspect of a dog-safe outdoor space. If you plan to leave your dog outside unsupervised for any length of time, you must have an ample and secure fence. Check existing fencing to make sure there are no gaps, and make sure all gates securely latch. Also, always double-check that your dog is wearing his identification tag every time before he is let out, just in case he does find a way to escape.

A good way to prevent backyard escapes is to stay with your dog. Try not to leave your Boykin Spaniel outside for extended periods alone. This dog was bred to work alongside humans in the field hunting, and it will not do well alone. A bored Boykin Spaniel is a mischievous one, and sometimes, that mischievous nature can cause trouble for both you and him.

Also, just like with indoor plants, some outdoor plants can be toxic as well. Check your outdoor plants and remove the potentially harmful ones before letting your dog explore.

CHAPTER 4

Bringing Home Your Boykin Spaniel

> "
>
> *Boykins will absolutely thrive and crush life in a highly structured environment, but will crumble and fail with tons of freedom too soon.*
>
> SCOTTY DUNNAM
> *Bluff City Boykin Spaniels*
>
> "

So, you've prepared your home and space for your new Boykin Spaniel, purchased all the supplies, and are ready to bring your new family member home! As pick-up day approaches and anticipation builds, you may find yourself a bit anxious, wondering how things will go, but if you follow the tips below, pick-up day should be fun, exciting, and trouble-free.

Picking Up Your Boykin Spaniel

Typically, when you arrive to pick up your puppy from the breeder, he or she will already be separated from the litter, awaiting your arrival. Try not to let the excitement of the moment distract you from getting all the information you need from the breeder!

Before leaving with your new Boykin Spaniel pup, the breeder should give you detailed information on your puppy's vet records, current shots, future shots, and deworming. They should remind you of any stipulations in the contract or health guarantee (as discussed in Chapter 2) and advise you on a feeding schedule. All this information, as well as breed-specific care tips, should be neatly presented in a packet of some sort, along with registration papers if applicable.

Sometimes, a breeder will allow you to take a small blanket or toy home with your dog so that the smell of his litter can comfort him during the transition. Ask ahead of time if this is an option so you will know if you need to provide the blanket or toy before pick-up day.

Photo Courtesy of Miles Arnette

The Ride Home

The first ride home with your new puppy can be daunting. It is your first time alone as a new family! Though you may be tempted to travel with your precious new puppy in your lap, it is safest to place your dog in a crate or a puppy harness for the trip. It is not uncommon for a puppy to get motion sickness and vomit on the way home, so you may wish to ask the breeder to withhold food the morning of pick-up day. You may also benefit from bringing a few extra towels just in case a mess needs to be cleaned up along the way.

Safe Travel Tips

If you are planning to transport your pup in a crate, know that not all crates will withstand the force of a crash, and some can even become more dangerous for your dog in the event of a crash. When not properly secured to the vehicle, the crate can become a projectile, injuring your puppy and possibly other passengers in the car. You can visit the Center for Pet Safety (CPS) website for a list of tested and approved travel crates.

If you are thinking of buying a harness for your dog to use in the car, know that they are not all created equally. The CPS performed a harness crashworthiness study in 2013, and results showed that only one of the 11 brands tested performed at the level advertised. Some were even deemed "catastrophic failures." Do diligent research on each brand before making your decision so you can be sure you get a safe harness.

No matter how you travel, always bring water and a bowl for your puppy; even if the drive is short, you never know when an unexpected delay, such as a flat tire, could occur, keeping you out much longer than expected.

Once you are all set up and prepared to leave with your new puppy, allow him to use the restroom on a patch of grass before loading him up. Praise him if he does, and begin your trip home! Try to make the trip home a positive experience for all. If your puppy is anxious, speak calmly to him until you arrive home. Those first few moments together can be scary, but they can also be a wonderful bonding experience for you both.

The First Night

As previously emphasized, you will want to have everything set up for your Boykin Spaniel so that you can focus all your attention and energy on bonding with your new pup. So, when it's time for the first night together, make sure his safe sleeping space is ready to go for him. Set up his crate with a crate pad or blanket in an area where you can hear him. While some find it easier to get up in the night and let the puppy out if he is in the same room, others feel they cannot sleep while the puppy is whining in their bedroom.

If you need to keep your puppy in a separate room, that is fine as long as you can hear him and are able to take him out to potty promptly when he wakes. Try not to move his crate around to different locations, as a predictable routine is most beneficial for both him and you.

At bedtime, there are a few things you need to do before crating your puppy for the night. Take your puppy outside and wait for 10 to 15 minutes for him to relieve himself. If the puppy does not, wait 10 minutes, and then try again. Repeat this process for however long it takes your puppy to go, and then put him directly into the crate for bed with his special blanket or toy from the breeder.

Your puppy will need to go outside to potty at least once during the night. It is best to take him out every time he wakes until potty training is well-established. When you take him out at night, immediately return him to the crate so that he knows nighttime is time for sleep and not play.

The first few nights home can be scary for your puppy, but this is normal. Remember, this phase is temporary, and before you know

Photo Courtesy of
Ryan Smith

it, you and your Boykin Spaniel will be in a routine that will make things easier. If your puppy spends the first night crying in his crate, you may be tempted to take him out and comfort him in your bed. This may seem like an easy solution, but it is best for everyone, including your puppy, if he learns early on to self-soothe in the crate.

Photo Courtesy of
Heather Beshears

If your puppy is having a difficult time sleeping in the crate or keeps you awake with his crying, try talking to your puppy or rubbing his head through the crate to help calm him. The most important thing you can do in the first few days is to make your puppy feel loved and secure. Bonds you form with each other in the early days will last throughout your dog's lifetime, and they will make all aspects of dog ownership that much more enjoyable. After a few nights, the bedtime whining should stop, and your puppy should come to find his crate a cozy place to sleep.

FUN FACT
Popularity

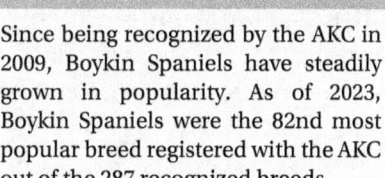

Since being recognized by the AKC in 2009, Boykin Spaniels have steadily grown in popularity. As of 2023, Boykin Spaniels were the 82nd most popular breed registered with the AKC out of the 287 recognized breeds.

The First Vet Visit

If your breeder has stipulated that you take your puppy to the vet within the first few days, you will need to make that appointment ahead of time so that there is no breach of contract. Be sure to take all records from the breeder to that first vet appointment. This appointment should be easy, as it is just a general wellness check-up.

Your Boykin Spaniel will likely be weighed, and the vet will examine his eyes, ears, nose, heart, and lungs. They will probably look at your puppy's coat condition and examine teeth and mouth. They may take a stool sample to check for parasites and keep the puppy up to date on vaccines if needed.

Take this opportunity to ask the vet any questions that may have come up about your puppy since you picked him up from the breeder. Don't be afraid to make a list ahead of time so that you don't forget anything. Remember, the only bad questions are the ones you don't ask!

Cost Breakdown for the First Year

When considering the cost of ownership for a Boykin Spaniel, it's important to look beyond the purchase price. While the purchase price is often significant upfront, there are several other aspects of ownership that will factor into the overall cost, and you will need to make sure you are financially able to care for all of a Boykin Spaniel's needs before making the decision to bring one home.

Besides the purchase price or adoption fee of your Boykin Spaniel, consider all the supplies you will need beforehand. Those are mentioned in detail in Chapter 3. Food costs can also be significant. Depending on the type and brand of food you choose, the cost can be up to $700 a year. Also, keep in mind the recurring costs, such as toys, chewable bones, beds, replacement collars and leashes, and anything else your dog may need.

If you are planning to hunt with your Boykin Spaniel, you will need to also account for training costs. Sending your dog to a training facility is the most effective and common way to teach him the skills he will need to accompany you on a hunt. These programs often last between three to six months and cost thousands of dollars, depending on the program. For quality training, expect to spend between $1,500 and $6,000.

> "
>
> *I am a believer in professional training, but not everyone can afford to send their dog to a training facility. By reading good training books, accessing online videos, and joining local hunting clubs, many individuals can pick up enough skills to work along with the dog's natural ability to be perfectly happy with their hunting partnership.*
>
> PATRICIA DOWNEY
> *Bayhill Boykins*
>
> "

Vet bills are another expense and probably the biggest one for dog owners. Depending on where you live, the office fee is about $50, and an exam can be upward of $100. A spay or neuter operation can cost up to $200. Vaccines are relatively cheap at between $20 and $30 each, but testing for anything from heartworm to diagnostic blood-work can cost anywhere from $20 to $250. If there is a more serious illness or injury, things can get incredibly expensive in a hurry. X-rays and ultrasounds can cost up to $300–$400. Anesthesia and sur-gery procedures for emergencies can run into thousands of dollars.

Photo Courtesy of
Reagan McColl

Pet insurance can help to offset some of these costs, but it can cost an average of $500–$600 per year.

Grooming is another necessary expense. A Boykin Spaniel doesn't need intense grooming, but a monthly bath and regular brushing are key. Invest in quality grooming tools to make the job easier.

If you are a traveler and plan to board your Boykin Spaniel occasion-ally, those overnight stays can be pricy, depending on where you live and which facility you choose. Even traveling with your dog can cost extra, so be prepared for those fees as well. Read more about traveling with your dog in Chapter 12.

Another cost some will need to take into account is a pet deposit. If you do not own your home, most landlords will require a hefty pet deposit before allowing a dog to reside there. Sometimes, these fees can reach into the thousands.

While some of these above costs are optional, many are required to properly care for your Boykin Spaniel and give him the life he deserves. If you have weighed the cost of ownership for a Boykin and believe you can responsibly care for one, this beautiful, hardworking hunting breed may be just the one for you!

CHAPTER 5

Being a Puppy Parent

Keeping Expectations Realistic

Becoming a puppy parent to a tiny Boykin Spaniel pup may be exciting, and rightfully so, but it's important you keep expectations realistic for the first few weeks. Don't let those adorable ears and eyes fool you: taking care of a puppy is a lot of hard work! There will be plenty of adorable "firsts" with your new Boykin Spaniel, but there will also be many frustrating ones. This chapter will go over all the potential puppy problems you may face and help you navigate them as smoothly as possible. If you put in the effort now, your Boykin Spaniel pup will reward you with a lifetime of loyalty, love, and obedience.

Potential Puppy Problems

No puppy comes without some level of frustration. It is like caring for a baby, after all. They need constant supervision and care and will undoubtedly test the limits and get themselves into mischief as they grow and gain independence. While each puppy will differ based on its particular personality, this section will outline some common complaints among puppy owners and help you better understand your puppy and correct potential issues.

Photo Courtesy of Cooper Holmes

Chewing

> *Boykins seem to be mouthier toward household objects and need training to teach them what acceptable toys are allowed. To make my point, Boykin owners call them 'Destroykins' instead of Boykins because of the many ways this breed discovers how to ravage supposedly indestructible toys, socks, dog beds, and other household items within reach.*
>
> ASHLEY COOPER
> *Silver Preferred Breeder*

Puppies chew on things; it's just what they do. Much like babies love to put everything in their mouths, puppies explore the world with their mouths as well. Chewing can also be a method of soothing sore mouths when teething pain strikes.

This behavior may be maddening at times, especially when it's your brand-new house slipper that has become the victim, but it's completely natural and inevitable. Never reprimand or punish your Boykin Spaniel for chewing. Instead, redirect him to something he can safely gnaw on and keep all the other items out of his reach. Try to supply him with ample chew toys or rubber bones that he can safely chew on. This allows your puppy to chew and protects the legs of your coffee table from harm.

If you catch your puppy chewing on something he shouldn't, remove the item or the puppy from the situation. Give him a stern "no," but don't punish him. Instead, use the positive "take and replace" method by giving him an appropriate chew toy instead. Never let your puppy chew on your fingers, as this can create a bad habit that is difficult to break once established.

Chewing due to teething will likely stop when all the puppy's adult teeth have grown in at around five to six months of age. However, some dogs just like to chew and will continue into adulthood. If your Boykin

Spaniel is a consistent chewer, you may want to invest in some bitter-apple spray. Spray this on anything your dog is chewing, and the bad taste should deter him. This spray can be especially handy if your Boykin has a fondness for electrical cords.

Photo Courtesy of Robert A. Miller

Jumping

> Limit their jumping in and out of vehicles and off furniture or jumping and twisting after bouncing balls or Frisbees to reduce the possibility of herniating a disc (IVDD genetic issues).
>
> **ROSLIN COPELAND & GINGER HURLEY**
> *Texas Trace Boykins*

The Boykin Spaniel is a highly energetic dog and will likely enjoy showing affection with an enthusiastic jump. Though your puppy means no harm, this behavior can lead to unwanted scratches or cuts to those on the receiving end. Nip this habit in the bud early with training so it doesn't become a lifelong battle.

When your Boykin Spaniel jumps up, give him a stern "no," then turn and ignore him until he settles. Repeat this over and over. It may take a while, but with persistence, your dog will eventually get the message and learn to keep his paws on the floor. Resist the urge to give him any attention, even by pushing him off you, as that may become a reaction he seeks.

Digging

Dogs dig for many reasons. Some dig out of boredom, some because they are hot and want to lie down in the cool dirt, and some for the sheer joy of it! Not all Boykin Spaniels will be diggers, but some may, especially if they aren't being exercised mentally or physically as they should. A bored Boykin Spaniel is much more likely to find himself exhibiting this unwanted behavior.

If your dog does take to digging, take precautions around your yard to keep both your dog and your lawn and plants safe. If necessary, you may need to fence off areas you do not want your dog getting his paws into, such as a flower garden.

If your dog is digging under a fence, try to determine why he may be doing it. Is there another animal on the other side demanding his attention? Is he bored and in need of stimulation and adventure? Ensuring your Boykin Spaniel gets the exercise he needs can help curb unwanted digging behaviors outside.

If you have a dog that just loves to dig holes, try a different approach. Let him outside under supervision only and watch him closely. Once he does his business, offer him a game of fetch or Frisbee to entertain him. If you notice him begin to dig, divert his attention to you and another game.

You might section off a portion of your yard as the "dig zone" and allow your dog to dig there safely. By allowing him a corner to dig, you may save yourself some flowerbed heartache. While it may not be ideal for you, it is a compromise to allow the dog to do what he loves in a less destructive manner.

Barking and Growling

Though it may sound intimidating, it is completely natural for Boykin Spaniel pups to bark and growl while playing with you or another animal. If you're in the middle of a spirited game with your new pup, and he lets out a vicious growl, worry not. It doesn't mean he is showing aggression. This is just the nature of puppy play and is exactly how he would be playing with his littermates.

If you want to discourage play fighting, don't do it by punishing your puppy. These are natural behaviors that should simply be ignored. Even an older Boykin Spaniel may bark and growl with you while playing. If your puppy or grown dog begins to play too rough and bark and growl, stop playing immediately and walk away. Come back when the dog settles down. If your dog continues to play too rough, repeat the process until your dog grasps the idea of what is and is not acceptable. This is exactly how another dog would teach a puppy his limits. It will take time, but it is well worth the effort.

If your dog seems truly agitated or begins nipping and biting in a way that seems defensive, it may be time to schedule a trip to see the vet. Truly agitated growling and biting behavior in a previously well-mannered dog can indicate a health problem that may be causing your dog pain.

Separation Anxiety

Boykin Spaniels love their people and are fiercely loyal. Because of their strong desire to be in their humans' company, they may struggle if left alone for long periods, especially without proper preparation or stimulation. It's important to understand that not all inappropriate behaviors when left alone are signs of true separation anxiety. Often, issues such as barking, digging, or chewing can result from boredom or a lack of adequate mental and physical stimulation, rather than separation anxiety.

Boykin Spaniels are high-drive dogs, bred for hunting and active companionship, which means they have significant energy and mental needs. Leaving a young Boykin Spaniel in a kennel for extended hours without exercise or mental engagement can lead to behaviors that might be mistaken for separation anxiety. It's essential to provide these active dogs with enough physical activity and mental enrichment before expecting them to settle calmly on their own.

For dogs that do need support when left alone, several strategies can help. Exercising your Boykin Spaniel before leaving the house can help tire them out, making them less likely to become restless. Offering an interactive toy, such as a treat ball or puzzle toy, can also help keep them entertained. This special toy should be reserved only for times when they are alone, which can help positively reinforce alone time as something enjoyable.

Photo Courtesy of Jennifer Berry

If you observe behaviors that seem extreme or persistent, such as excessive barking, pacing, or destructive acts, and other strategies don't help, it's wise to consult your veterinarian. They can help determine whether true separation anxiety is at play and provide guidance on appropriate treatments or strategies to keep your dog comfortable during short absences.

Crate Training

> *The first routine I'd work on would be kennel training. I recommend 30-plus minutes with the dog in the crate, taking it outside to use the bathroom, 30ish minutes playing, and then putting it back into the crate. This allows the puppy time to play and learn the proper place to use the restroom, and the understanding that it will not always be out while you are out. This habit also begins potty training your puppy. Puppies only need about one ounce of water per pound of weight per day.*
>
> JONATHON GRABARA
> *Tradewater Kennels*

Dogs are not true den animals by nature, but they do need a safe and quiet place to retreat to when they feel scared or anxious. In the wild, dogs and wolves only den when they rear puppies. These dens are usually holes dug in the ground by the mother wolf. The holes are abandoned when the puppies are old enough to travel with the pack. Although the ancestors of domesticated didn't spend their days in a den, that doesn't mean your new puppy won't find comfort in a "den" of his own in your house.

Crate training can be controversial among animal lovers. Some believe it to be inhumane and too cage-like. Others believe a crate is a necessary training tool used to protect and secure a dog. The fact is using a crate for training makes puppy ownership more convenient for you and safer for your pup. When done properly, crating your dog is an excellent tool for house-training and will set your dog up for success from the beginning.

There are multiple crate options to choose from—plastic, wire, soft shell, and heavy-duty. The two main crate types are plastic and wire. If you're planning to travel with your Boykin Spaniel, you will need a plastic crate, as this is the only type the airlines allow.

Another common crate type is the wire crate. These allow more visibility and airflow for your dog. These crates are typically collapsible and are easily stored when not in use. Depending on the size, some wire crates come with a divider to section off the crate. This is a nice feature that allows for a smaller puppy to grow into a larger crate so that you don't have to purchase multiple crates as he grows.

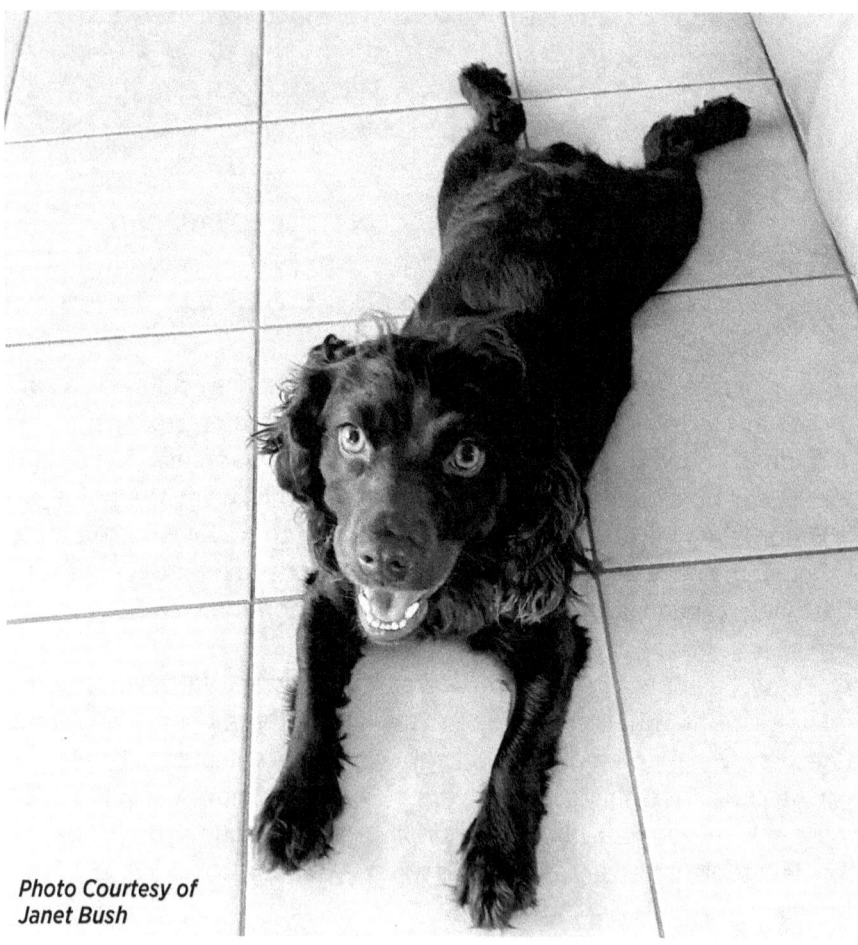

Photo Courtesy of Janet Bush

Whichever type you choose, line your crate with a commercial crate pad or with a towel or blanket for comfort. You want the crate to be inviting and become a comfortable spot for your Boykin Spaniel to retreat voluntarily.

HELPFUL TIP
Family Dogs

Boykin Spaniels are excellent family dogs due to their friendly and affectionate nature. In addition, these little brown dogs are known to be wonderful, energetic companions to children. Boykin Spaniels were initially bred as retrievers, so they have a higher-than-average prey drive. Still, they can adapt to living situations with cats or other small pets if adequately socialized.

The key to successful crate training is positive reinforcement. Do not ever put your dog in the crate as a form of punishment. This sends the message that the crate is a bad place and will create issues going forward. You don't want your dog to view the crate as a "timeout" box, or he will never retreat there willingly.

The first time you introduce your new puppy to the crate, you'll want to have some training treats on hand. Secure the door of the crate to the side so that it doesn't accidentally swing closed and scare your puppy. Begin by placing a treat or two outside, near the door of the crate. Depending on how your dog reacts to the crate, slowly place the treats closer until you can put one inside. Your puppy should voluntarily go inside the crate to get the treat.

Don't shut the door of the crate the first few times the puppy goes in. Instead, praise him and allow him to come in and out of the crate freely. After your puppy becomes comfortable with the open crate, guide him inside and gently latch the door. Give him treats from outside the crate and verbally praise him. Only leave him in there for a few moments at first and stay with him. This will help him feel comfortable. Practice this exercise the first day you get your puppy home to get him comfortable with the crate before his first night in it.

Any time you need to crate your dog, do so by rewarding him with treats and a special toy. Praise him and make it a fun experience to get inside the crate. Don't leave your dog in the crate for long the first few times, except for nighttime, or he may begin to get anxious and associate those feelings with the crate. Practice leaving your puppy in the crate while you're home for short increments of time, 30 minutes to an hour. Always immediately take your dog outside to his potty area when you let him out of the crate, even if it hasn't been long.

Be sure to exercise your dog thoroughly before expecting him to have any crate time. It is not reasonable for you to put your dog in a crate without first allowing him to expend his energy. Doing this will allow him to rest and sleep in his crate while you're away, further minimizing the chances of separation anxiety.

A crate is a tool that needs to be used responsibly. Never leave your Boykin Spaniel in the crate for an extended period. Also, never treat the crate like a dog-sitter. With proper training, your puppy will outgrow his need for the crate and will no longer need to be confined to it while you're sleeping or away. If your puppy doesn't view the crate as a place of rest and comfort, you may need to reevaluate the way you're using it.

Leaving Your Boykin Spaniel Home Alone

> *Boykins need and must have structure and boundaries. They also need consistency; the crate should be their safe space, not a prison cell. They should go in the crate when you eat dinner, watch TV, and do other activities not just when you leave the house. They must earn free time, as too much freedom is detrimental.*
>
> ERIC GRUBBS
> *Bar 6 Boykins*

Leaving your Boykin Spaniel alone for the first time can be nerve-wracking for both you and him. Plan ahead and be sure to get your Boykin Spaniel well acquainted with the crate before you leave him alone for the first time. Play with him vigorously or take him for a long walk just before it's time for you to leave so that he will be more likely to lie down and nap while you're away.

When it is time for you to leave, follow the same guidelines previously mentioned. Reward your dog with a treat for entering the crate, and give him a special "crate-only" toy as an additional reward and boredom buster. Interactive treat toys like Kong work great for this.

When you return from your first trip away, it may seem fitting to greet your puppy with an excited hello, but refrain so that you don't make your dog think getting out of the crate is more exciting than going in. Going in the crate should be fun and exciting, and getting out should be no big deal. Open the door with little fuss and promptly take your dog outside to do his business. This will help keep your dog from becoming overexcited every time you let him out of the crate.

Crate training is a process, and it takes both time and effort. Some dogs take to the crate easily, and some need a little more time and practice. Your Boykin Spaniel will not like to be left alone, as they are high-energy companion dogs. This means it is highly important that you do not overuse the crate and make the dog associate it with the negative feelings of being left alone. If you do need to regularly leave your dog home alone, reconsider getting a Boykin Spaniel, as that is not a life he will enjoy.

CHAPTER 6

Potty Training Your Boykin Spaniel

Potty Training Methods

There are two basic training methods employed by trainers—positive reinforcement and negative reinforcement. More information about each of these methods can be found in Chapter 10, but it is important to know that the best way to potty train your Boykin Spaniel is through positive reinforcement. You may have heard to "rub your dog's nose in it" when he's had an accident, but we now know that not only is that method ineffective, it's a cruel punishment for a puppy who doesn't know better.

The goal of potty training is to teach your puppy that your home is also his home. Instinctually, dogs will not soil the places where they eat and sleep. So, until your dog is potty trained, you will need to keep him confined to a small, controlled area of your home so he does not go off into an unused corner to relieve himself. This controlled area could be a puppy playpen in the same room as you when you first begin potty training. As potty training progresses, you will be able to expand the areas your dog can go until, eventually, he may have the run of the house—if that is what you desire.

Take your puppy out often, about every hour, and reward him freely with verbal praise and treats. Try to consistently take him to the same area so he will smell his scent and know that it's time to potty. Make this time with your puppy calm and all about the business. Do your best to ignore his attempts to play until after he's finished so that he doesn't forget the reason he went outside in the first place.

It may take 10 to 15 minutes, but when your dog relieves himself, celebrate enthusiastically and reward him with a training treat. This will help show him that going potty outside is a positive and fun experience. Your Boykin Spaniel puppy is highly trainable and wants to learn, so when he begins to understand that relieving himself outside is what you want, potty training should be a breeze.

Photo Courtesy of Robert M. Harris

Using the Crate for Potty Training

> "
>
> *Potty training and crate training are crucial for a puppy to be successfully integrated into a new family. Take the puppy outside often and out of the same door. I hang a bell from that door handle and teach the dog to ring the bell when it needs to go outside. Later, it will let you know when it has to go outside. Crates are a necessity. Dogs are denning animals. They will eventually want to spend free time and sleep in their crates, and that way, they won't be left in situations that will get them in trouble. The first few weeks, especially at night, can be tough, but hang in there. It will eventually get better.*
>
> MARK LEE
>
> *Holland Ridge Boykins*
>
> "

The crate is a great tool to use for potty training because it allows you to control your puppy in a small space during the times you can't supervise him. If you're using a wire crate, install the divider inside so that the area is big enough for your dog to comfortably stand and turn around but not big enough that he can take several steps to the other side. This will prevent him from soiling one side and sleeping on the other.

A good rule of thumb to follow for a young puppy is for every month old he is, that's how many hours he can wait to go potty. That doesn't mean that you should only take your puppy out that often because if you do, you will most likely be cleaning up a lot of accidents. This is simply a guideline for how long a young puppy can be left in the crate before he must go out. Never leave your puppy or dog in the crate longer than four to six hours, except at night.

When morning comes, immediately take your dog outside to the designated potty area. If you're planning to put your dog back into the crate while you're gone for work, make sure he has plenty of time outside of the crate and take the time to exercise him thoroughly before you do.

This will help your dog rest better while you're gone. You will need to come home to let your dog out at lunchtime. Follow the same procedure before putting him back into the crate. However, this is not an ideal life for a Boykin Spaniel. If you plan to leave your dog in the crate while you are away at work often, you should reconsider ownership, as this breed will not enjoy being left alone daily.

If you must leave your dog on a daily basis, consider puppy day-care instead. Not only will this allow you to socialize your dog, but it will also be a fun place for him to play and use up his energy while you are away. Usually, these places require certain vaccinations, so be sure to call and check ahead of time. If doggy daycare is not an option, call a friend or family member to come by and let your puppy out for you, or have them keep him during the day. You can even hire a dog walker to come and exercise your pup while you are away. Go through a reputable

Photo Courtesy of
Jennifer Berry

service like Care.com so you can read references and know they've had a background check.

If you absolutely must leave your dog in the crate or a puppy-proofed room for longer than you should, you can use a puppy pad on one side of the crate. This will slow down the training process because you will, at some point, have to remove the pads and retrain your dog that the only acceptable place to go is outside. Again, if you will be consistently leaving your Boykin Spaniel in the crate for extended periods of time, you should consider the well-being of your dog and explore other options. This breed loves companionship with humans and will be unhappy if left to spend most of the day alone.

The First Few Weeks

> 66
>
> *When your new Boykin puppy wakes up from a nap, take it outside to potty. The moment it loses interest in playing, take it out for a potty break. If you are crate training, take the puppy out for a potty break before and after putting it in the crate. Before the dog goes to bed, take it out to potty. Potty breaks are the dominant theme during the first few weeks at home, and it can be exhausting! However, establishing a routine potty schedule sets the expectations for your new puppy, and it will be house-trained more quickly.*
>
> ASHLEY COOPER
> *Silver Preferred Breeder*
>
> 99

As previously discussed, the first few weeks with your new Boykin Spaniel puppy will be a transition period for both of you! Don't let anyone tell you potty training a puppy is easy. Potty training takes time and patience and probably a few bottles of carpet cleaner. Despite the challenges the first few weeks present, know that there is light at the end of the tunnel. Through the frustrations and accidents, your puppy will eventually figure it out, and your life together will become much more enjoyable with a lot less frustration!

Potty training begins the day you bring your Boykin Spaniel pup home. In the beginning, take your dog out every 45 minutes to an hour during daytime hours. He may not need to go every time, but give him 10 to 15 minutes to try. Even if you have a fenced backyard, it will benefit you to take your dog outside on a leash. This will allow you to control where he goes and help him not to be too distracted. This may seem like an inconvenience to you, but it will be worth it, as the consistency will help him learn that potty time is outside.

Rewarding Good Behavior

> *You'll need to accompany your Boykin puppy outside for all of its potty breaks. Due to the breed's strong desire to be by your side at all times, the dog will often remain by the door on your deck or patio instead of eliminating or having a bowel movement. I learned this the hard way with my first Boykin. It took me about a week of cleaning up multiple accidents to realize I had to accompany the dog on potty breaks. The advantage of this is you can train the dog where you want it to potty in your yard.*
>
> TABBY LANGLEY
> *Tabby's Sweet Boykins*

Remember, positive reinforcement is the best way to teach your Boykin Spaniel. This essentially means you are rewarding your dog for doing the right thing instead of punishing him for the wrong action. So, don't forget to praise him verbally and with a treat as soon as he finishes going potty outside. Remember, your Boykin Spaniel wants to please you, so if you can effectively communicate what you want from him and learn to read his signals, potty training should come much easier.

How to Handle Accidents

> "
>
> *House-training is critical, and it is heavily your responsibility to set the pup up for success. Do not leave the pup unsupervised in any room of your home. If you are not directly watching the dog, put it in the crate. A good trick we have found is if you want to relax and watch TV, leash the puppy to you and you will know when it begins to stir and sniff about. Also, house-training happens one room at a time. Gradually enlarge the area of your home as a potty safe zone as the puppy becomes successful.*
>
> PATRICIA DOWNEY
> *Bayhill Boykins*
> "

Learning to potty outside is a big deal for a little Boykin Spaniel puppy and will require patience from you and him. Unfortunately, accidents are going to happen! It just comes with the territory. So, go ahead and buy yourself a bottle of odor-neutralizing cleaner beforehand.

If you have been trying to train your dog to go on the grass, accidents on rugs and carpets are inevitable. The feeling of the carpet on a dog's paws is very similar to the feeling of grass and can sometimes trick a young puppy into thinking he can relieve himself there. If this becomes a problem, you might want to temporarily remove any rugs from your puppy's designated area until he gets the hang of going outside. Keeping rugs rolled up neatly in the garage can save you lots of frustration and money!

When you catch your Boykin Spaniel in the moment of an accident, quickly pick him up and take him outside to the potty area. Don't punish or yell at your dog; simply give a stern "no" and take him outside. Remember, accidents are inevitable and are often the result of the owner not taking the puppy out as often as he needs. Still, sometimes a dog will soil the carpet a mere minute after coming inside. Regardless, your Boykin Spaniel pup is still learning and should not be punished for the mistake, as punishment will only cause confusion and prolong the potty-training process.

Doggy Door Pros and Cons

Doggy doors can be beneficial in your effort to potty train, especially for an older Boykin Spaniel. If you have a secure backyard, a doggy door can allow your dog to let himself out as he pleases. This could mean fewer accidents and a shorter training period. You should never let your dog go outside unsupervised unless you know the backyard is completely

Photo Courtesy of
Thad Frazier

secure and your dog can't escape. Adding a doggy door is not for everyone and does come with risks. You should review this list of pros and cons before making your decision.

Installation: Installing a doggy door is making a permanent change to your home, and they are notoriously difficult to install. If you don't own your home, a doggy door is probably not an option for you.

Unwanted Visitors: Doggy doors are great for allowing your dog to freely come in and out of your home, but they may unintentionally offer that same freedom to unwanted wild animals as well. A doggy door could become an entry point for a thief or even a much smaller masked bandit, like a raccoon! Buy one with a locking function to avoid this issue at night.

Indoor Cats: If you have an indoor cat, it will be nearly impossible to keep him from leaving through the doggy door. If your cat has been declawed, this is particularly dangerous because your cat will have no defense from predators. If you have an indoor cat who already loves to go outside, a doggy door will allow him to bring his "treasures" inside the house. Finding a dead snake or bird in the house is probably not what the doggy door was meant for.

Securing the Yard: Before allowing your dog unsupervised time in the yard, you must be sure it's a safe area. Be sure the fence is secure, and add a lock to any gate so neighborhood kids or thieves cannot let your dog out. If your dog is a digger, then you may have a problem with him digging out to go explore.

Backyard Pool: Another danger to consider in the backyard is a pool. Even though your Boykin Spaniel is a fantastic swimmer, he should never be allowed near the pool unless you are out there with him, just in case of an accident. Swimming alone is dangerous, even for a dog like the Boykin Spaniel.

If you allow full access to the pool, your Boykin Spaniel will likely swim often, as this breed loves the water! A doggy door permits your dog to come in and out freely while sopping wet, causing a big mess for you to clean up when you get home.

Fire Escape: One positive to a doggy door is it allows your dog to escape the house in case of an emergency. This could potentially save your dog's life in the event of a fire.

If you know your yard is safe and secure, and you want to install a doggy door to aid in training, go ahead! You will need to confine your dog's indoor privileges to a small space while still allowing access to the doggy door. This can be done by using a playpen set up against the wall.

HELPFUL TIP
Apartment-Friendly

Due to their size, Boykin Spaniels are an excellent choice for apartment living. However, because their energy levels can be pretty high, there may be special considerations for this living situation. Regular exercise, such as daily walks and playtime, is essential to stimulate them physically and mentally. Potty training may also present some unique challenges. Consider crate training, establishing a routine, and taking frequent outdoor breaks.

A doggy door is not always a good option, but in the right scenario, it can be very helpful. For elderly or disabled owners who have a more difficult time getting around, a doggy door allows the dog to relieve himself in the proper area without any burden on the owner.

If you decide on a doggy door, be prepared for a little bit of training; your puppy will not know how to use it otherwise. The first time you teach him to use it, give him a gentle push through and have another person on the other side ready with a small treat and plenty of praise. Do this several times in both directions. Once your puppy allows you to push him through without resistance, go to the opposite side of the doggy door, extend your hand through to the puppy, and allow him to smell the treat in your hand. Use the treat to lure him through. Finally, call him from the other side, and give him a treat when he goes through by himself. If you spend five or 10 minutes a day doing this, your Boykin Spaniel should be going through the door by himself within a week.

CHAPTER 7

Socializing Your Boykin Spaniel

Why Socialization Matters

> "
>
> *Socialization is not just the process of acclimating your Boykin to only one thing. It consists of taking and doing things in a variety of different environments. This may include tall grass, loud noises, people, places, other animals, boats, golf carts, anything that you can envision your puppy being around for the rest of its life.*
>
> JONATHON GRABARA
> *Tradewater Kennels*
> "

Boykin Spaniels are highly social dogs and do well with both people and other dogs if properly socialized from an early age. By beginning your dog's socialization early, you can be sure that he will be able to thrive with any people or dogs he encounters in any environment. This will make life easier for you and for him, as he will inevitably encounter other humans and animals regularly throughout his life, whether it be on a hunt, a stroll through town, or even at a restaurant.

Your Boykin Spaniel will be naturally social, so teaching your puppy proper social etiquette and manners is of high importance to training a well-behaved dog, especially if you plan to hunt with him.

Behavior around Other Dogs

> "
>
> *I recommend exposing your puppy to safe dogs you know very well early. Do not take your dog into public places or around other dogs unless you know for a fact that they are good with puppies.*
>
> EDITH HINES
> *Woodland Holler Boykins*
>
> "

As you probably know, dogs have their own code of social etiquette, which is much different from ours. Imagine if people greeted each other the way dogs do by sniffing, circling, and jumping up and down playfully. That would be a silly sight! Luckily, our social rules are a bit stricter than theirs. However, dogs understand these behaviors a little differently than we do, and oftentimes, dog-to-dog behaviors that we may find strange are completely normal.

Much like people, dogs greet each other differently at a first meeting than they greet an old friend. Oftentimes, these encounters depend on the individual dog's personality as well. Dogs typically greet each other in one or all of the following ways:

Sniffing: Probably the most notable canine ritual is the sniff test. When dogs greet one another, they may begin with the muzzle or go straight for the backside. Sometimes, the sniff will be brief, and sometimes, it can seem like a full-blown investigation. Unless one dog seems uncomfortable, this is perfectly normal behavior and doesn't need to be stopped. Once the dogs have satisfied their sniffers, they can move on to the next step in the canine greeting.

Play Stance: Have you ever seen a dog approach another dog and immediately go into a play bow? This behavior is simply one dog attempting to initiate play with another. It's like he's saying, "Hey there! Do you want to be friends and play together?" Even a quick, playful growl accompanied by a friendly tail wag is acceptable. Again, as long as neither dog seems stressed, there is no need to stop this behavior. Even if the other dog declines the offer to play, that doesn't mean the meeting was not positive.

Exerting Dominance: This greeting is probably the least endearing, but it is still acceptable in the canine world. One dog may exert his dominance by being the first to sniff and by non-aggressively showing the other dog he is in charge. This could include mounting. This process may be obvious to you, or it may all happen so quickly that you don't even notice until one dog rolls over to show his belly in submission. As with the other behaviors, these are the natural social ways of dogs and should not be stopped unless there is real aggression or stress. Dogs take social cues well and are pretty good at keeping each other in line. If one dog is not satisfied with another's behavior, he will probably let the other know.

Photo Courtesy of Theresa Miller

Knowing these common dog behaviors and greetings can help you determine how things are going when your Boykin Spaniel is socializing with other dogs. Learning to read your dog's behavior can help prepare you to know when you may need to step in and separate the dogs. Safety is always the key when socializing.

Safe Ways to Socialize

> "
>
> *Allow a two- to three-second sniff of a new dog and then recall your Boykin for a reward for a positive interaction. Make this a practice for greeting new dogs, even when they are adults. Because Boykins are described by the AKC as being cautious, it's important all owners be aware of this trait and respect their dogs' need for personal space if their behaviors are indicative of the need.*
>
> ASHLEY COOPER
> *Silver Preferred Breeder*
>
> "

Puppies, especially energetic Boykin Spaniel puppies, are playful and social by nature. This makes puppyhood the perfect time to begin socializing your Boykin Spaniel, as he will likely be eager to meet other playmates and be adaptable to new situations. Socialization should begin as early as possible, but be sure not to allow your puppy to have close contact with dogs you don't know until he has had his complete series of puppy shots.

There are different opinions on how socializing with other dogs outside of a controlled environment, like in a puppy class, should be done. Some professionals believe all first greetings should be done with restraints or barriers, just in case. Others believe these barriers and restraints cause stress for all dogs involved and can elevate the tension. They believe that dogs that are allowed to freely greet each other can do so more comfortably without feeling trapped.

If you choose to socialize your puppy with a leash on, keep your puppy close on a leash or on the other side of a barrier, such as a gate, when you make introductions with other dogs, especially those that are older or larger. Preferably, all other dogs should also be leashed or somehow restrained in case something goes wrong.

Allow the dogs to greet each other for a few seconds and then walk away. At this point, each owner should distract their dog until it is no longer interested in the other dog. If the initial interaction goes well, allow the dogs to come together again in the same manner. Keep the leash loose so your dog can maneuver but not so loose it becomes a tangled mess. Read each dog's body language to determine how the greeting is going. Bodies should be relaxed, and there should be no staring contests. As the dogs become comfortable and relaxed with each other, you will be able to let them off-leash, and they can have supervised play.

If you choose the no-leash method, make sure all first greetings are done in a neutral location so that no dog can feel territorial and defensive. Allow the dogs to meet, but monitor their body language. If they use the body language described above, you don't need to interfere. But if either dog seems stiff, uncomfortable, or agitated, separate the dogs and use distractions to get their attention off each other. Off-leash greetings

can bring a greater risk if you don't know the other dog well and should only be done with friendly, pre-socialized dogs. Safety is the most important thing when socializing your dog, so only do what you feel comfortable with.

If you are dealing with an adult Boykin Spaniel from a rescue center, you may be in for a more challenging job. Depending on his prior socialization, he will likely need more time and extra patience as he adjusts to his new life and home with you. He may

HISTORICAL FACT
Don't Rock the Boat

Boykin Spaniels originate from South Carolina, a state crisscrossed with rivers and swamps. As a result, Boykins are especially well-suited to this unique environment. In addition to their webbed feet, Boykins' small size made them ideal boat companions for eager hunters. In contrast to Labrador Retrievers, which commonly weigh 70 to 80 pounds, Boykin Spaniels are half this size and can perform many of the same hunting and retrieving maneuvers.

have experienced some trauma in his life that causes challenges when socializing with other dogs. Often, with a rescue, you don't know exactly what his life has held up until the point he was rescued. He may have been kept in a cage his whole life, been abused by his owner, or even been previously attacked by another dog. All these things are unknowns that could have a significant impact on the dog's social abilities.

Allow your Boykin Spaniel to socialize on his own terms, even if it is in small increments. Avoid putting your dog in situations that cause him more stress, as this will not help him but rather hinder his progress. Together, you and your Boykin Spaniel can overcome these challenges and build a strong bridge of trust.

If your Boykin Spaniel is reluctant to socialize, begin the process at home. Take your dog on a walk through the neighborhood so he can see other dogs but not necessarily interact with them yet. With much time and persistence, he should eventually become comfortable enough to walk past other dogs in their backyards or on leashes without becoming stressed. When he has successfully mastered these indirect encounters, it's time to move on to the next step.

If you have a neighbor with a dog, this is a great place to start direct socialization if they are willing. These dogs will probably encounter each other at one point or another and will benefit from getting to know each other. Ask your neighbor to arrange a time to allow both dogs to meet in a neutral part of the yard. Take things slow and give the dogs space if either seems stressed. Follow the three-second rule and then walk away and distract each dog. Allow the dogs to come together again if the first encounter went well. If it doesn't seem to be going well, that's okay! Allow the dogs to just be in the yard at the same time until they become used to each other, and then gradually allow them to interact more as it seems appropriate.

If you don't have a neighboring dog, call a friend or family member with a dog. If the dogs get along well, try to set up regular playdates so that your Boykin Spaniel can continue to work on socialization skills. Weekly walks at the park together or even off-leash playtime at each other's homes may be possible once the dogs get to know each other.

A dog park is another option to meet other dogs, but it's not the best one. These parks can be overwhelming, especially if they are crowded, and they are notorious for unpleasant encounters. Additionally, dog parks can be unsanitary, posing health risks to young puppies that are not yet fully vaccinated. For these reasons, dog parks should be considered a last resort for socialization, and only after ensuring your puppy has completed all vaccinations.

If you must visit a dog park, begin by just walking around the perimeter at a comfortable distance. Listen to your dog, and take his cues. If he seems comfortable, allow him to interact more closely with a dog through the fence. If he remains calm, praise him. Reward him for positive encounters and remove him from negative ones. Try to only let him interact with dogs that are also calm. It will not help the situation to engage with a loud, barking, rambunctious dog through the fence. This could cause stress for an unsocialized dog and stop progress.

More important than progress is comfort and security for your dog. He needs to feel safe with you above all, and if that means socialization progresses slowly, it is better to take baby steps with a challenging Boykin Spaniel than to cause him undue stress by trying to force him into social situations he isn't ready for. Remember, a sociable nature comes naturally to a Boykin Spaniel, so if he is struggling to coexist with other people and animals, he likely has some significant trauma in his past.

Socializing With New People

> It is critical before a Boykin puppy turns 16 weeks old to fully socialize it with dogs, people, and other animals. The socialization starts with the breeder. Ask your breeder what steps/actions are being taken to socialize your puppy even before you bring it home.
>
> AUDRA BOYKIN
> *Legacy Boykins*

Just about everyone loves greeting a puppy! They are just so hard to resist when you see them out in public. Getting your Boykin Spaniel puppy used to people should be relatively easy, considering how outgoing and fun this breed is. In fact, the biggest challenge you will face when introducing your puppy to new humans is likely going to be jumping. While it may seem cute now, this habit is difficult to break if you allow it early on.

Ideally, when approached by a person, your puppy should remain calm and keep all four paws on the ground. If you need to stop a jumping habit, begin by teaching your dog an alternate command. "Sit" is a good command to combat jumping because your dog can't do both at the same time. When your dog gets overly excited and begins to jump, counter by giving the "sit" command. Reward him for sitting and staying calm. If he can't stay calm and continues to jump, leave the room as suggested in Chapter 5 and ignore your dog for 30 seconds to one minute. Return and try again. This process works well for meeting new people, getting the leash out for walks, or any other exciting event that gets your dog jumping.

Again, an unsocialized adult Boykin Spaniel may have a more difficult time accepting new people, depending on his past. If your Boykin Spaniel has social challenges and seems nervous around humans, begin new introductions slowly so as not to stress him too much. You and anyone you introduce him to will need to work to earn his trust, and depending on his past, that may take much time and patience.

If you're having guests over, ask those people ahead of time to remain calm and not show the dog much attention. This may help ease your dog's mind and keep him calm. If your guests want to rub and love all over your pup, even with the best intentions, it could cause him to become overexcited and stressed. Once calm and comfortable, the dog may be trusting enough to allow a belly rub or two, but it should always be on his own terms. Give your guests some training treats to gain his trust. If your dog is particularly shy and nervous, and you don't see much progress being made, try separating him with a baby gate so that he can observe the people but not feel pressured or overwhelmed.

Other ways you can socialize your dog are by taking him out to dog-friendly stores and meeting people. Big-box hardware stores are a great place for this. They are typically dog-friendly and full of people who will find it hard to resist the urge to ask you about your Boykin Spaniel! Have a few small treats handy and ask people to give one to your dog—he will quickly learn that meeting people is a good experience.

Photo Courtesy of
Heather Beshears

Boykin Spaniels and Children

> **"**
>
> *Do not leave a puppy and children unsupervised by an adult. Use gates and crates to achieve this goal. Puppies can get dropped and injured accidentally, and children can get nipped and scratched by little needle teeth. Your goal is to develop a healthy relationship between the pup and the children. This can only be done under direct supervision.*
>
> PATRICIA DOWNEY
> *Bayhill Boykins*
>
> **"**

The Boykin Spaniel is a great family dog and does well with children. If introduced at an early age, your Boykin Spaniel should have no problem at all spending his time around kids. In fact, he will become loyal and loving to them, just as he is to you!

If you wish to further strengthen the bond between your Boykin Spaniel and your kids, allow your children to take an active role in his training. Give them some training treats and show them how to teach the "sit" command, as described in Chapter 10. Not only will your puppy learn to respect your children, but your children will learn patience and other valuable life lessons!

No matter how good your Boykin Spaniel is with your kids, for everyone's safety, it is important to always closely supervise any dog-to-child socialization. This is simply good dog parenting. An excited Boykin Spaniel shouldn't show aggression toward kids but is more likely to accidentally cause injury with a friendly, enthusiastic jump. This is another reason to nip that habit in the bud as early as possible.

Always teach your children to be gentle and kind, never pulling ears, hair, or tail. Show them by example the proper way to pet your Boykin Spaniel so that they understand how to handle him safely. No matter how friendly and trustworthy your dog is, never leave a child and dog alone unattended. This is for the safety of both the child and the dog.

CHAPTER 8

Introducing Your Boykin Spaniel to Other Pets

Introducing a Puppy to Existing Pets

Introducing your Boykin Spaniel to other pets, including cats or other small animals, is very different from dog-to-dog introductions. Certain precautions should be taken to make sure the meeting goes well, and all animals are safe. It is possible for your Boykin Spaniel to have positive relationships with other species, but these relationships should start as early as possible, preferably as soon as you bring your puppy home.

When introducing your Boykin Spaniel to a resident cat, begin by keeping your puppy and cat separated. Place a blanket or toy with the puppy's scent near the cat. Do the same for the puppy in a different area of the house. Let the dog and the cat sniff and become accustomed to the scents before a face-to-face interaction.

After exchanging scents, allow your pets to interact indirectly. Keep them separated by a gate or the crate, but allow them to view each other. Depending on their reactions, you may feel comfortable enough to let them loose, but be careful—your puppy probably can't do much damage to your cat (depending on his age and size), but your cat can definitely harm your puppy if he feels threatened.

Try introductions with someone gently holding each animal. Let the two sniff and explore, but watch carefully for claws. Praise both animals for calm and reasonable reactions. Stop the introduction immediately if any fear or aggression is shown.

Most likely, your Boykin Spaniel pup will want to make friends with your cat and play right away. Your cat, on the other hand, probably won't know how to handle all of his playful energy and curiosity and will need a place to escape. This escape should be off the ground in an area where your dog can't reach. Always allow your cat to leave the situation whenever he needs to.

Though the Boykin Spaniel is an avid hunter, his skills lie in retrieving, so he does not have a strong chasing instinct. This makes him more easily compatible with other smaller animals in the home. Still, it is always best to keep any very small and vulnerable pets away from dogs just to be safe.

Photo Courtesy of Amanda Lamm

Introducing an Older Boykin Spaniel

If you have adopted or are planning to adopt a mature Boykin Spaniel, make sure he does well with cats before bringing him home to one. If the shelter or the rescue center knows that he does not get along well with cats, it is best to keep looking and let that dog go to a home without a cat. There is no need to stress an adult dog by introducing him to a home with other animals if he prefers to be an only pet.

Introductions for a mature Boykin Spaniel and a cat need to be done carefully, as an adult dog can cause potential harm to a cat and vice versa. Begin with the same scent exchange described above. After a day of letting the animals get accustomed to each other's scent, allow the two to meet through a closed door. Depending on individual

*Photo Courtesy of
Kristen Booker*

personality, either pet may not be very interested in the other, or the animals may be busting down the door to see who is on the other side. Allow each animal to become calm and relaxed before any face-to-face interactions.

Once the two have become relaxed and calm on both sides of the door, allow the animals to meet with the dog on a loose leash. Allow a brief interaction before separating them and diverting their attention. If the initial interaction was calm and peaceful, try again. If you decide to let the two interact with your dog off-leash, always ensure your cat can escape to his safe space, designated just for him.

Cats and dogs can live peacefully together and can even form close bonds, but it may not happen overnight, and that is okay. Just because it takes time doesn't mean your pets won't eventually have a tight-knit relationship.

Fighting/Bad Manners

As previously mentioned, Boykin Spaniels are generally cheerful and friendly with other dogs and people. Aggression is not a common issue for this breed; however, despite proper breeding and good genetics, improper treatment or a traumatic past can cause aggression issues in any dog. This is why understanding how to deal with aggression is especially important for anyone considering bringing home a rescue Boykin Spaniel with an unknown history. Understanding possible triggers and reactions can help you better understand your dog and help him overcome the obstacles he faces so you can live together in harmony.

If your dog displays any aggressive behaviors, such as growling or snapping, the first thing you should do is take him to the vet to rule out any underlying conditions. Sometimes, unbeknownst to the owner, a dog can actually be in pain, which causes him to become irritable and react aggressively in certain situations. Treating the underlying pain can help your Boykin Spaniel stop the aggression altogether.

Once this is ruled out as a cause, evaluate your dog's current situation. Is something causing him stress? A life change? Is he being left alone too long? Are you meeting his energy requirements and his need for companionship and adventure? This breed was bred to hunt with

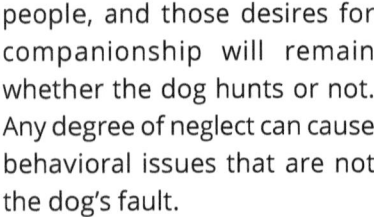

people, and those desires for companionship will remain whether the dog hunts or not. Any degree of neglect can cause behavioral issues that are not the dog's fault.

If your Boykin Spaniel is showing aggression toward other dogs, it may be a lack of proper socialization. Go back to Chapter 7 and learn how to socialize your dog safely. Dogs dealing with aggression issues may progress slowly, so take your time and don't rush your Boykin Spaniel into a situation that could cause setbacks or even injure him or another dog.

If your dog is showing aggression toward other pets at home, begin by identifying the

HELPFUL TIP
Boykin Spaniel vs. American Water Spaniel

The Boykin Spaniel and American Water Spaniel are two distinct breeds that can be difficult to distinguish at first glance. Both breeds are small, brown, official state dogs known for their excellent swimming and retrieving abilities. However, despite similar coloring and size, these breeds' most significant visible difference is their coats. American Water Spaniels have thick curly to wavy coats designed to help them withstand the harsh Wisconsin winters, while Boykin Spaniels have flatter coats with slight waves. Another distinguishing feature of these breeds is their tail. Boykin Spaniels typically have docked tails, while American Water Spaniels have longer, tapered tails with feathered fur.

source. Food aggression is a common issue among pets at home. Does your dog become possessive of toys or treats? If you identify the source of aggression, remove it.

If your dog is dealing with food aggression, eliminate the situation by feeding your dog in another room or crate, away from all other pets. Crate feeding is especially helpful if you have multiple dogs, as it reduces food aggression and reinforces the crate as a positive environment. It also allows you to closely monitor each pet's food intake, ensuring that none of them overeat or, conversely, refuse to eat—either of which could require a visit to the veterinarian. If your dog is particularly possessive of a favorite toy, only allow him to have the toy within the confines of his crate or designated alone area. Removing your dog from the stressful situation will not solve the aggression problem, but it will make life easier while you deal with the root cause.

If your dog isn't causing any physical harm to you or any other members of your family, continue to work on carefully socializing the dog and rewarding friendly behavior with treats and praise. If the aggression doesn't improve or evolves to physical harm in any way, seek a professional trainer's help immediately. Never leave a potentially aggressive dog alone or unrestrained with another animal or an unfamiliar person.

When Is It Aggression?

Dogs frequently growl and bare their teeth when they play. This is totally normal behavior and does not automatically mean your dog has aggression issues. The truth is, sometimes it can be quite difficult for us humans to distinguish between play and aggression.

When your dog and another dog are playfully bowing and taking turns chasing, rolling over, and mouthing each other, these are all signs that they are engaging in play together. This type of play should be encouraged, as it offers your dog valuable life experience and social lessons. This type of play helps your Boykin Spaniel practice his social skills and is a wonderful outlet for excess energy.

However, if the dogs are playing, but one or both seem stiff and tense, there may be more than a playful romp going on between them. Deep, drawn-out growling, staring into the other dog's eyes, and a one-sided chase may all be indications that one or both of the dogs are showing some real aggression, and you may need to end the encounter.

If you feel your Boykin Spaniel is playing too rough or becoming aggressive with you, simply walk away and ignore him. In a pack of dogs, older dogs will naturally teach the younger pups when enough is enough. They do this with a verbal cue, and then they end play immediately. Even puppies of the same litter do this to each other.

As the owner, you can take the same stance. When play becomes too rough, give a loud verbal "yip" and walk away, ignoring your dog. After a minute, once the dog seems to have shifted his attention, return to play. Repeat this process until the dog understands that rough play is not acceptable. Eventually, he will understand the reason you keep walking

Photo Courtesy of
Becky Stanley Preston

away and will lessen his intensity. After all, it was not his intent to harm you. He is still learning his boundaries.

Also, be aware of how you approach your dog for play. If you come in swinging and throwing your hands and arms around, this is encouraging your dog to play rough. Use toys instead of your body, and keep movements gentle.

What to Do When Pets Don't Get Along

If you've exhausted all the above tips and your pets simply can't seem to get along, call a professional and get help. Don't hesitate, as the situation could escalate quickly and lead to injury. The sooner you address the aggression with a trained professional, the easier it will be to overcome.

If you find yourself in a situation needing to break up a fight between dogs, you need to know how to do so safely so that you are not harmed in the process. Use the wheelbarrow method by grabbing each dog by the back legs and pulling them apart. You will need two people restraining the dogs for this method.

If you are alone and cannot use the wheelbarrow method, grab two metal pots and bang them against each other to make a loud noise. This should startle and distract the dogs long enough for you to separate them before the aggression continues. Water also works well to distract them. If you are outside, grab the hose and spray both dogs to distract them so you can separate them physically.

Never put yourself between two fighting dogs, no matter how much you trust them. This could likely lead to injury, even if they do not intend to cause you harm.

CHAPTER 9

Exercising Your Boykin Spaniel

How Much Exercise Does a Boykin Spaniel Need?

> "
>
> *Exercising a Boykin is actually rather easy if you teach them to love retrieving. I take mine on two 15-minute walks per day. We have two or three retrieving sessions each day, lasting about 10 minutes each. Once you have trained your dog to sit, stay, come, heel, and any other cute tricks you want it to learn, then you might consider agility training. It satisfies the physical and intellectual training the breed needs.*
>
> **TABBY LANGLEY**
>
> *Tabby's Sweet Boykins*
>
> "

The Boykin Spaniel is highly energetic and needs significant amounts of exercise to remain happy and healthy. This dog was bred to be outdoors and active, and that is what he loves to do the most. If you cannot devote at least one to two hours of outdoor exercise to your Boykin Spaniel each day, you need to reconsider getting one, as he will suffer mentally and physically without it.

If you are looking for a dog to join in on an already active lifestyle, the Boykin Spaniel is the one for you! This breed is a perfect companion for the outdoorsman and will provide excellent company on nature walks, hikes, neighborhood jogs, and, of course, hunting.

Though the Boykin Spaniel requires a very active lifestyle, it is important to note puppies must be exercised gently as their joints are not fully developed until the age of about 18 months. Swimming, gentle walks, and playtime are best for a puppy's developing joints. Rigorous hiking and jogging long distances are better suited for mature Boykin Spaniels.

Photo Courtesy of Mitchell Hall

Easy Ways to Stay Active

> **"**
>
> *Once your Boykin is old enough, take it for walks, but not too far while it is young; you need those growth plates to close before long walks, but walking is great. Throwing a tennis ball for retrieving is also great, but the best exercise (in my opinion) is swimming. It's easy on the joints, the dogs keep cooler than running around on land, and you can join in. Lakes, ponds, pools—Boykins love them all. But keep in mind that they can drink too much water while swimming and get water toxicity.*
>
> DAWN CRITES
> *Lily Pad Spaniels*
>
> **"**

As previously mentioned, the Boykin Spaniel would love to accompany you for your morning jog, a walk through the park, or even a trek on more rugged terrain. That isn't all he's suited for, though! This spunky little ball of fur is particularly adept at agility. It seems that all those traits that make him an excellent huntsman also lend him superior agility skills.

If you are looking for an exciting and easy way to keep your Boykin busy, both physically and mentally, start agility training. Agility training doesn't have to be complicated; it can begin by simply teaching your dog some fun basic agility commands, such as spinning and jumping through a hula hoop. After mastering these at home, start setting up other pieces of a course, and before you know it, you and your Boykin Spaniel will be accomplishing new feats and achieving new goals together as a team. Of course, you can also seek out a professional agility training class to attend with your dog if you want to take the sport more seriously and compete.

Teaching Your Boykin Spaniel to Spin: Start with a training treat and a verbal cue, such as "spin." Begin by getting your Boykin Spaniel to face you and give you his attention. Give the verbal cue, then hold the treat to his nose and let him follow it all the way around as you prompt him to spin. Reward him with the treat and a verbal "yes." Continue this until he begins to spin with just a simple verbal cue.

Teaching Your Dog to Jump Through a Hoop: Begin by placing the hoop on the ground and calling your Boykin Spaniel over to check it out. Reward him for coming close and stepping inside the hoop on the ground. Next, stand the hoop up, still touching the ground, and lure your Boykin through to the other side with a training treat. As you call him through the hoop, give a verbal cue such as "through." As he becomes comfortable with this, raise the hoop off the floor a few inches at a time until he is jumping through on command.

If agility isn't your thing, it's important you find other ways to keep your Boykin Spaniel active. While outdoor activities are imperative, there will sometimes be days when a jog or a hike isn't an option. Maybe the weather is poor, or an injury keeps you down temporarily. Try some of the following ideas to help you and your dog get past a rainy day or an exercise slump.

FUN FACT
Webbed Feet

One of the unique attributes of the Boykin Spaniel is its webbed toes. These little flippers play a critical role in the Boykin Spaniel's swimming and retrieving abilities, enabling the dogs to paddle efficiently through the water. They have an affinity for water and are generally adept swimmers.

Use a Flirt Pole – A flirt pole is basically a stick with a toy attached to the end with a string. It allows you to engage your dog in a game of chase without much movement of your own. You can even use the flirt pole from a seated position. A flirt pole can be a perfect solution for an owner who has temporarily limited mobility and cannot run alongside their dog. The flirt pole engages your dog mentally and physically—a win-win!

Play Hide-and-Seek – Once your dog has mastered basic commands and can sit and stay, try engaging him in a game of hide-and-seek. Take your dog to a chosen location in the house and have him sit and stay where he is. Then, go hide elsewhere in the house and call him when you are ready.

If your dog won't stay still long enough to allow you to hide, try giving him a treat that will take him half a minute or so to finish. Once he finishes, call out from your hiding place and see how long it takes your Boykin Spaniel to find you. Keep giving him encouragement until he figures out where you are. The game is fun for you and him alike and is a great way to give your dog exercise on a rainy day!

Play Fetch – So simple, yet so effective. There is not much a dog loves more than a game of fetch. Play with a tennis ball, rope, Frisbee, or a training bumper—especially a bird-shaped one if your Boykin will be hunting. You can even attach wings to the bumper to make it both fun and practical training for your Boykin Spaniel. Mix it up to keep things interesting, and your spunky little Boykin will love it! Teach your dog to return the item to your lap, and this game can be a consistently easy outlet for excess energy.

Scavenger Hunt – A typical dog has up to 300 million olfactory receptors in his nose, and the part of a dog's brain devoted to smell is proportionally 40 times larger than a human's. That means your Boykin Spaniel has a powerful sniffer! Make mealtime or snack time fun by creating a game out of it and putting that nose to work.

Hide small amounts of food or treats around a room and see if your dog can sniff them out. If you hide them in enough areas, he may find himself running around the room from spot to spot, trying to find the sources of the smell. While this may not provide as much exercise as some of the previous suggestions, it is still a way to keep a bored dog entertained on a dreary day.

Dog Daycare – Even if you spend most of your time at home with your dog, an occasional trip to a local dog daycare is a great way to give your pup some playtime with other dogs while also allowing you to run errands without leaving your Boykin Spaniel alone. After a few hours at daycare, your dog will likely be ready for a relaxing nap at home.

Importance of Mental Exercise

> *Boykins are smart and loving. Our crew love going for boat rides to islands where we toss bumpers in the fresh water for them to fetch. They will do this all day, so remember they get tired and hot (they have dark coats), and you are the adult and need to protect them. We always have shade available and only do focused training that involves running in the cooler mornings or evenings. Note that, like most dogs, they will swallow saltwater, so be sure to limit saltwater exposure and be ready with fresh water.*
>
> **SHAWN MARIE DOUGHERTY**
> *SOHO Edition Boykin Spaniels*

Physical exercise isn't the only kind of exercise your Boykin Spaniel needs. Keeping your dog's mind active and sharp is just as important! Not only will it keep him sharp, but it will prevent him from becoming bored and destructive.

Many of the suggestions in the previous section serve as both mental and physical exercise. Learning agility, playing hide-and-seek, doing scavenger hunts, and using a flirt pole all provide a high amount of direct mental stimulation, as does interacting with other dogs at dog daycare. However, there are other things you can do with your Boykin Spaniel to stimulate him mentally as well.

There are toys and puzzles made specifically for dogs with the intention of keeping their minds busy. These are great for times when you are away or simply too busy to engage with your Boykin Spaniel. Kong makes a range of toys that can keep your dog occupied for a long time and are basically indestructible. A favorite is the Classic Dog Toy. This is a rubber toy with a hollow center made for stuffing with treats. Kong has a line of treats and snacks, or you can simply fill the toy with peanut butter. The Kong toys are dishwasher safe and cost between $8 and $25, depending on size, making them a great, affordable option.

Another option is a dog puzzle. The Trixie Poker Box has four compartments, all covered by a lid. Your dog must figure out how each lid can be removed to get the reward waiting inside. All four lids open differently, so this will take some real focus and determination on your dog's part. Once your Boykin Spaniel figures out the trick to opening all boxes, this puzzle may not present a challenge anymore. So, keep the toy in your arsenal for the occasional day when your dog must be left alone.

Tips for a Bored Dog

The Boykin Spaniel is a spunky little companion dog, ready for any adventure that involves his people. This breed is bred to work in the fields alongside humans, and the dogs will suffer without dedicated companionship. If you plan to leave your Boykin Spaniel alone for periods of time often, consider another less needy breed. That said, every dog must be able to handle being alone at times without becoming distressed or bored.

As mentioned above, one great thing you can do to keep a dog occupied while you're away is to leave him with an interactive toy or puzzle. Another option is an electronic device that you can control and interact with your dog through a mobile device, such as a phone.

Photo Courtesy of Pamela Parton

Clever Pet is one of these devices. This is a unique system that challenges your dog with sequences, memory games, and electronically released treats or food when solved. This system comes with a light-up pad that shows different colors and patterns. Clever Pet is designed to progressively get more challenging as your dog figures it out. Use the mobile application to track progress and monitor use. This system is wonderful for dogs who are left alone for long periods of the day. It comes with a $250 price tag, but it is worth it if it means you don't have to spend money cleaning up after a bored dog.

The iFetch Frenzy is another option. Not as high-tech as the original iFetch, which is electronic and can launch a tennis ball up to 30 feet, the iFetch Frenzy uses gravity instead of electricity to drop the ball through one of three holes and send it rolling across the floor. Once your dog learns to return the ball to the top, he can play solo fetch for hours while you are away.

When Boredom Leads to Destruction

A bored dog is a destructive dog. If you find that your Boykin Spaniel is becoming destructive, evaluate his typical level of stimulation. Is he getting enough physical exercise? Is he lonely and in need of more companionship? Or is he simply bored and in need of some mental stimulation?

No matter the reason, a bored and destructive Boykin Spaniel should not be punished. He is simply reacting to his circumstances the only way he knows how. Try some of the above tips and tricks, and your problems will likely be solved.

CHAPTER 10

Basic Obedience Training for Your Boykin Spaniel

Benefits of Basic Obedience Training

> *I tell everyone, 'Train the dog in front of you.' Dogs, just like people, have different personalities. Some are bold, courageous, and outgoing, while some are timid and shy. Training your new puppy should take these traits into account.*
>
> JONATHON GRABARA
> *Tradewater Kennels*

A well-trained and obedient dog is invaluable, and the benefits of obedience training are endless. Not only will training together strengthen the relationship between you and him, but it will help keep your dog safe in times of crisis. A properly trained Boykin Spaniel will come when called and will obey any command out of trust and loyalty.

Obedience training isn't a one-size-fits-all. You have options when it comes to basic beginning training. You can attend a group obedience class, hire a personal dog trainer either at a facility or in your home, or do it yourself. If you plan to hunt with your Boykin Spaniel, it is important that you train intentionally and consistently so that your dog may seamlessly transition into fieldwork-specific commands when the time is right.

Training at Home

Many people choose to train their dogs in their own homes. Training your Boykin Spaniel yourself is possible and rewarding if you do it properly. Whether you train your dog yourself or you prefer to hire a professional trainer, training in your own home is a great way to fit training into even the busiest of schedules. Also, it allows you to begin training earlier while protecting your young puppy from potential virus exposure in an obedience class.

There are drawbacks, however, to training at home. One is not seeing how your dog reacts in less-than-optimal situations. If all training takes

Photo Courtesy of Amanda Ard

place in the distraction-free zone of your home, your dog may not know how to react when there are distractions around. And there will be plenty of distractions, whether in the field or on a neighborhood walk. You need your dog to obey in any situation, at home or outside, where there are potentially dangerous distractions everywhere. In a group class setting, your dog is learning to be obedient regardless of what is going on around him, and this is an invaluable skill.

When training at home, it is good practice to occasionally take your dog somewhere else to practice obedience with real-life distractions. If you hire a trainer, ask how they make sure to train your dog in all situations and ask about the possibility of taking a training field trip to a public place. This option gives you the best of both worlds while also ensuring proper training.

Maintaining Clear Expectations

Regardless of whether you choose to train at home or in a group setting, such as an obedience class, it's important you maintain clear expectations. This will set you and your Boykin Spaniel up for success from the beginning. Your Boykin Spaniel will be eager to please and willing to learn any new command you wish to teach him, so your training sessions should be enjoyable. Persistence and positivity will pay off immensely.

If you choose to attend obedience classes, either private or group, there are a few things you should know ahead of time. These classes are usually held once or twice a week, and most facilities require you to provide vaccination records before classes begin. Obedience training typically begins at six months of age, but dog ages in a class can vary widely. It is never too late to start obedience training, so even if you have a senior Boykin Spaniel, he's not too old to learn!

Before your first training session, ask what is provided and if there is anything you should bring. The facility will likely require your dog to have a leash and may ask you to provide your own training treats. Most obedience classes require a name tag with identification, and some require a clicker. By purchasing all necessary supplies before the class, you can ensure that all your time is spent learning from the trainer and not scrambling to get what you need.

No matter how frequent obedient classes are, be prepared to spend a minimum of 15 to 20 minutes daily working on what your dog has learned. Just as with any skill, obedience training takes practice and repetition. Show him patience as he learns and reinforce good behaviors positively.

Photo Courtesy of
Bethany Barmes

Basic Commands

> "
>
> *It seems most hunting breeds become bored when performing basic obedience commands over and over. I believe that Boykins, being such versatile dogs, are willing to participate in repetitive basic command training because they like to work and it's like it becomes their job to work in unison with the owner. A new owner should know that all Boykins are different because genetics create differences in personality, temperament, and depth of interest in activities. However, with enough training, encouragement, and hard work, some of the most difficult aspects of training can become possible.*
>
> ASHLEY COOPER
> *Silver Preferred Breeder*
> "

Obedience training is not just about learning to sit or shake; it's about building trust between you and your dog and building a foundation for further training in the future. Learning how to communicate your wishes in a way your dog can understand is the goal. A great way to build this trust is by teaching your dog basic commands.

Most obedience classes or personal trainers will begin the training by teaching a few easy, basic commands. If you are choosing to be the trainer yourself, follow the steps below to master these five basic commands.

Sit – The sit command is the easiest one to teach and can be learned in a short period of time. Take your dog to a calm area that is free of distractions like toys. Have a bag full of very small training treats ready. With your dog standing facing you, hold a treat in front of his nose and slowly raise it up and over his head so that he is forced to sit down and look up. Give the verbal command "sit" as you do this. When he sits, reward him with a treat and a key phrase such as "yes" or "good." If you're training with a clicker, also give a click when he obeys the command.

Down – Once your dog has mastered the sit command, move on to the down command. Guide your dog into a seated position, facing you. Hold a treat in front of his nose, lower it to the floor, and give the verbal command "down." If your dog raises his backside to a standing position to retrieve the treat, take the treat away and say "no." Begin again from a seated position. When your dog successfully lies down to retrieve the treat, reward with a treat, a positive verbal cue such as "yes" and a click.

HELPFUL TIP
Mental Training

Boykin Spaniels are known for their sharp minds and quick learning abilities. As a result, these dogs often enjoy puzzle toys that require problem-solving skills. These toys range from treat-dispensing puzzles to games requiring your dog to manipulate doors or move objects to access rewards. By providing your dog with interactive puzzle toys, you can stimulate his mind while teaching him important concepts like patience, persistence, and critical thinking—all of which will help you in your training and obedience endeavors.

Heel – Teaching your dog to heel requires him to walk on your left side at your pace whenever you're out and about. The heel command is a bit challenging and requires significant focus from your dog. He must stop when you stop and walk when you walk, never stepping in front of your left heel. This command is great for preventing leash tugging.

Begin by having your dog sit in front, facing you. Using your left hand, let your dog smell the treat and then swing your arm around to the left, luring your dog to turn around and stop in a position next to you but slightly behind, facing the same direction you are. Reward your dog immediately when he arrives in the correct position. Use the command "heel." Repeat this command many times, always having your dog come to the heel position before rewarding him.

After your dog has mastered the heel position, progress by taking a few steps using the same verbal "heel" command. Reward your dog for walking with you in the correct position. If your dog leaves the correct heel position, guide him back to where he is supposed to be before continuing.

Stay – To teach your dog to stay, command him to sit facing you. With a visible treat in hand, hold out your palm to your dog and say, "Stay." Take one step backward. If your dog doesn't move, quickly return and reward him. You don't want your dog leaving the stay position to retrieve the treat. If your dog moves, say "no" and return him to a sitting position. As your dog gets the hang of "stay," increase the number of steps.

Leave It – This command is valuable and can help keep your dog safe if he gets into something potentially dangerous. Begin with two treats, one in each hand. Keep one hand in a fist, but allow your dog to sniff the treat. As your dog tries to get into your hand to get the treat, verbally command him to "leave it." Repeat this command until your dog backs off, and then reward him with the treat from the other hand. As your dog progresses, make the treat more accessible and challenge your pup to "leave it" in exchange for another treat.

Methods of Training

> "
>
> *Boykins can get bored easily. Make sure you keep them focused and don't drag training out. Let them have three successful responses and then stop. You can repeat this multiple times during the day, but keep each individual training session short.*
>
> DAWN CRITES
> *Lily Pad Spaniels*
>
> "

There are two main methods when it comes to training a dog: alpha dog training and positive reinforcement. Hotly debated among dog trainers, these two methods are vastly different. When choosing the method that is right for your dog, you must take some things into consideration and understand the details of each one.

Alpha Dog Training

> ❝
> *Boykins respond well to formal and informal training using simple and consistent terms. They learn quickly and love a gentle pat and positive words of reinforcement. Negative reinforcement can be dangerous, especially if inconsistently given. An owner should expect a Boykin to be enthusiastic about training and eager to understand and meet its owner's expectations.*
>
> SHAWN MARIE DOUGHERTY
> *SOHO Edition Boykin Spaniels*
> ❞

Alpha training, popularized by television dog trainer Cesar Millan, focuses on making yourself the alpha or the leader of the pack. This training begins early by maintaining heavy control over your dog's actions. Users of this method are told to never allow their dog in their bed, not to let a dog go through a doorway before they do, and never to get down at eye level with the dog. It is also advised that people touch their dog's food to get their scent on it before giving it to him and not to let the dog eat until the owner gives the verbal okay.

Proponents of this method claim that dogs are pack animals and need to have a sense of who is alpha in order to learn to submit. They claim that wolves will assert their dominance over one another to keep each other in check, and they attempt to achieve the same dominance by using highly controversial methods. However, research has shown that wolves in the wild actually do not have such a rigid hierarchy. They live socially among each other, much like humans do with our own families. Also, cross-species dominance has not proven successful at any point in history.

When it comes to obedience training, alpha training employs the use of restraints such as choke and shock collars and forceful body maneuvers. This method relies heavily on punishments and teaching your dog what he is doing wrong rather than teaching him how to do it right. While some trainers believe in the effectiveness of alpha training methods, others believe it is cruel and can undermine your relationship with your dog, making it one based on fear and not trust. This method of training is absolutely not suitable for a Boykin Spaniel.

Positive Reinforcement

> **"**
>
> *Boykin Spaniels are very quick to learn basic commands. Naturally, praise is the top motivation for the dog to learn any command. The addition of a small treat also helps with training, but after the skill is learned, the treat should just be the praise.*
>
> NANCY DICKSON
> *Sunstar Kennel*
>
> **"**

The most widely accepted and recommended method of training today is positive reinforcement. The idea is that by reinforcing good behavior and obedience with desirable treats and praise, your dog will learn the commands and build trust with the trainer. It is still important to let your dog know that you are in control, but this is done through positive reinforcement rather than force. Bad behavior is not punished by harm or discomfort; rather, it is ignored or redirected until the positive behavior becomes consistent. It is about helping your dog understand what you want him to do so he can do it.

Dogs have been selectively bred over thousands of years to live alongside humans. They thrive on companionship and will typically do anything to please their people. Using positive reinforcement is a method of teaching them to understand what you want them to do and teaching them that what makes you happy also makes them happy. This is the opposite of fear-based training and will build loyalty and trust naturally.

When training using the positive reinforcement method, there are two types of reinforcements used: primary and secondary.

Primary Reinforcement

Primary reinforcements are directly related to the innate basic needs your dog has. These include things such as food and water. Training treats are a primary reinforcement successfully used in training. Make sure you use specific training treats, as they are typically small so that your dog can train with them longer without being overfed. Many trainers also use small bits of deli meat as a high-value reward.

Secondary Reinforcement

Secondary reinforcements are not based on instinctual, basic needs but on cultural constructs. This includes verbal praise, smiles, and pats.

Your dog must learn to associate these actions positively by pairing them with primary reinforcements.

Another type of secondary reinforcement is conditioned reinforcement. This is when something neutral, such as a whistle or a clicker, is used in conjunction with a primary reinforcement to create a positive association. Conditioned reinforcements can be highly effective initially but can lose their effectiveness when the primary reinforcement is taken away for an extended period.

Dangers of Negative Reinforcement

> *Praise to a Boykin Spaniel is like a treat ... They live for that loving touch or kind word from their owner and respond immediately. Harshness or scolding is not recommended for a Boykin pup. The pup is sensitive and could withdraw if put in an environment where harshness and seclusion are prominent.*
>
> NANCY DICKSON
> *Sunstar Kennel*

Correcting by punishment, as is used in alpha training, has no scientific research backing it up as a legitimate training method. This type of control over a dog can lead to fear and anxiety in the animal and can even put you or your family in danger. Using this method without an experienced professional's supervision can lead to a damaged relationship with your dog and a loss of trust.

Not only is this type of training risky, but it is also often ineffective. Your dog almost never does anything "bad" intentionally. He is aiming to please, and if he is disobedient, it is most likely because he has not been taught what he is supposed to do. By punishing your dog when he does something undesirable, he will often be hurt and confused by what has happened. He may never fully understand which action was the reason for his discomfort in the first place.

Instead of punishing your dog to stop him from doing what he isn't supposed to, show him what he *is* supposed to do and reward him for that. It may take a little bit longer to master, but your relationship will grow positively in the process.

Photo Courtesy of Michelle Hansen

When to Hire a Trainer

If you are attempting to train at home but aren't making progress, it may be time to hire a professional trainer. Training a dog takes a lot of time and consistency, and it is easy to get frustrated, sending your dog mixed messages while training. If the mixed signals go on for too long, it can cause major setbacks in your dog's progress. If you are dealing with any kind of aggression or poor social behaviors that do not seem to be improving with work, hire a trainer specialized in that area to help you get through to your dog. If you think you need help from a professional trainer—don't put it off. The sooner your dog is properly trained, the sooner you can live together in peaceful companionship.

CHAPTER 11

Hunting and Fieldwork

If you are looking for a Boykin Spaniel, it's likely you have hunting in mind. If that's the case, you may be wondering where to begin with hunting and fieldwork training. This chapter will review the ins and outs of how you take that sweet little fur ball from a pup to a master in the field.

At What Age Does Fieldwork Training Begin?

> *Get your Boykin interested and retrieving as early as possible. We want to enhance that prey drive as early as possible. Do not focus on the dog being steady when getting the dog interested in retrieving; just get the dog going and wanting more and more. If you see the dog losing interest after four retrieves, stop at two or three. You have to keep the dog wanting more. Remember, it's a process built one day at a time. If the dog fails at something, it's probably because it's unclear what's being asked. Break it down and try again. Always end on a positive/ good note. Never stop on a failure. And do not take the dog hunting too early. Nothing good comes from pushing a dog too fast.*
>
> **SCOTTY DUNNAM**
> *Bluff City Boykin Spaniels*

As mentioned in the previous chapter, basic obedience training must happen first as it will lay the foundation for fieldwork training. This basic obedience training should begin early, at around two to four months of age. Along with basic obedience, early and frequent socialization is crucial for a future hunting dog.

Take your future hunting companion with you everywhere you go and get him or her exposed to all sorts of sights and sounds. Because your Boykin Spaniel will need to be accustomed to loud sounds such as gunfire, be sure to make plenty of noise on occasion so your Boykin will get used to it from day one. Stomping your feet or banging some pots together may seem silly in the beginning, but it will pay off later in the field.

There is no concrete age for when your Boykin Spaniel should begin fieldwork training. Rather, it depends more on your individual dog's readiness. Once the foundations of basic obedience training and socialization have been laid, many choose to begin fieldwork training from six to twelve months of age.

Photo Courtesy of
Robert M. Harris

Introducing Water and Gun Sounds

> "
>
> *Acclimate your new Boykin to everything that you feel it may encounter in the future. Also, Boykins are Spaniels. Building prey and retrieving desire is mandatory. Far too many times you see new owners holding their puppies back to make them 'steady' or showing off the hundredth retrieve they have done for the day. Retrieving is a game. It must be fun for you and the dog. In the beginning, one to two throws a day may be more than enough.*
>
> JONATHON GRABARA
> *Tradewater Kennels*
>
>

Even before official fieldwork training begins, it is crucial that you introduce your Boykin Spaniel to water and gun sounds as early and often as possible. Your Boykin Spaniel will be spending plenty of time in the water on hunts, so introducing it in a fun and positive way will make training easier for you and him.

When introducing your Boykin Spaniel to the water as a very young pup, only allow him to wade in very shallow water. Once your pup is old enough to swim safely, around four to five months, take him to a small pond with a gradual entry. If your pond has a steep drop into deep water, this may startle your Boykin Spaniel upon entry. The last thing you want to do when introducing your dog to the water is to associate it with any amount of fear, as this will be challenging to overcome and could hinder training in the future.

Allow your Boykin Spaniel to investigate the water of his own will. Be prepared with the proper attire to enter the water yourself, too, as this will help to show your Boykin Spaniel that the water is safe and help him build confidence. Never toss your Boykin Spaniel into the water to make him swim, as this will create negative associations.

If your Boykin Spaniel doesn't jump in and swim on the first outing to the pond, that's okay. This should be a gradual process that will build

*Photo Courtesy of
Tommy Reeves*

each time you go out. Eventually, your Boykin Spaniel will be making water entry on command, so try not to worry if he seems hesitant the first time out.

Introducing your Boykin Spaniel to gunfire needs to be done gradually, starting as soon as possible. Ideally, acclimation begins with an audio program once the puppies' ears open. This type of program combines music with gradual introductions of gunfire, allowing them to adjust comfortably. By the time the puppies are ready to go home at around eight weeks, they should already be familiar with the sound of a .22. It is important to continue this acclimation process rather than pausing for several months. Be sure to check with your breeder about what steps they have taken to introduce gunfire. When you are ready to continue introducing gunfire at home, do so while engaging your puppy in activities they love, like eating or playing, to create positive associations.

Begin by choosing an activity your Boykin Spaniel loves. Playing fetch is a good one. Just before you throw the dummy, clap your hands loudly. After a few rounds like that, introduce another sharp, loud noise,

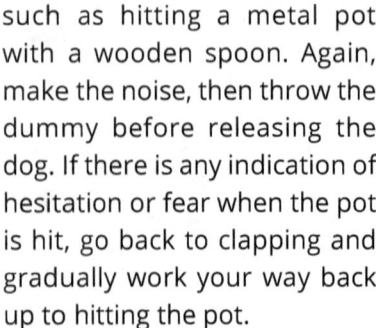

such as hitting a metal pot with a wooden spoon. Again, make the noise, then throw the dummy before releasing the dog. If there is any indication of hesitation or fear when the pot is hit, go back to clapping and gradually work your way back up to hitting the pot.

Once your dog is unfazed by the spoon hitting the metal pot, it is time to introduce the .22 caliber shot. Using the exact same method, fire a .22 blank before you throw the dummy and release the dog. Again, if

HELPFUL TIP
Daily Retriever Work

Boykin Spaniels have a moderate to high energy level, so take advantage of their natural propensity for retrieving objects. For example, your Boykin is likely to enjoy interactive games like fetch. You might even consider investing in durable, floating toy balls and a doggy pool for your backyard to take advantage of your dog's retrieving and swimming skills simultaneously. These games are a great way to bond with your new companion and channel his energy in a fun and fulfilling way.

there is any indication of fear, put the gun away and go back to the metal pot until your Boykin Spaniel is ready.

As you can see, the point of this method is to gradually introduce a louder and louder sound to your Boykin Spaniel while he is doing something that he enjoys, such as fetch. These progressions should happen over a period of days or even weeks, not all in one training session. With patience, your Boykin Spaniel will be fearless of the gun in no time and ready to take on the field.

Boats and Blinds

If you want to teach your dog to hunt from a boat, you will, of course, need to get him accustomed to the boat. Just like when introducing your dog to the water, you will need to introduce him to the boat slowly.

Begin with the boat on dry land near the water. Get into the boat yourself and call your dog into the boat with you. Reward him with a training treat when he comes into the boat. Get in and out of the boat together until your dog is comfortable and confident.

Photo Courtesy of Austin Boyd

After your dog is comfortable getting into and out of the boat, give him a retrieve off the boat onto dry land. Do not go directly into the water, as this may be off-putting to your dog. Once he has mastered the retrieve from the boat onto dry land, transition him to retrieve off the boat, onto land, and then into the water. So, from the boat, throw the dummy into the water and let your dog go from the boat to the land and then into the water. Eventually, you will transition from the boat directly into the water. Again, this process is meant to span days or weeks, not just one day. With patience and persistence, your Boykin Spaniel will be ready to accompany you on a boat in no time.

If you will be using a field blind, teaching your dog to use it properly will serve you well in the field. This skill is important for success as well as safety, so practicing it often until it is mastered is crucial. Training your dog to stay in the blind until called for a retrieve will keep him out of the blast zone and safe from harm.

Your dog should already know the kennel command before you attempt to teach him to use the dog blind. Begin with the blind outside, giving your dog the kennel command. Help him to get into the blind if

Photo Courtesy of Cooper Holmes

he is reluctant. Training treats can be useful here. Once in the blind, praise him and then call him back out and repeat. Getting your dog used to the blind can take time, so practice is important! Practice this skill outside or even inside in the living room.

Photo Courtesy of John Haddrick

Once your dog is comfortable in the blind, send him in and give the sit command. Let your dog practice waiting in the blind until you give the retrieve command. Put your dog in the blind and throw a dummy. If your dog comes out early, push him back in, correct him, and do not let him retrieve that dummy. Reset and throw another dummy.

Basic Hunting Commands

The basic hunting commands overlap somewhat with simple basic obedience, which is a good thing! If your dog has already learned basic obedience commands such as sit, stay, come, and heel, then he is ahead of the game. These commands will be the building blocks for the next skills he will learn.

In addition to basic obedience commands, it's important to introduce whistle commands and hand signals during obedience training. These cues are invaluable for hunting and will help your Boykin Spaniel respond at a distance. Your dog will also need to learn a release word, which can be anything from "release" to "go on" or even his name. Choose a release word that won't accidentally be spoken in the field, potentially causing confusion for your Boykin Spaniel.

Photo Courtesy of
Shelby Wagenseil

Flushing

Flushing is when your dog is trained to find and "flush out" the prey. The dogs use noise and movement to startle the birds into the air. Boykin Spaniels are known for their keen flushing abilities.

When training a dog to flush, many trainers will use a whistle or verbal commands to signal their dog through a flushing pattern. This looks somewhat like a zigzag through a field. It is the same basic commands used when teaching flushing: sit, heel, wait, and release.

Flushing dogs are prized for their ability to get birds moving quickly before they can move into safer cover. They will flush, sit when the birds are in the air, and then retrieve when released. When properly trained, flushing dogs are invaluable in the field.

Training Your Boykin Spaniel to Deliver to Hand

> *I introduce the puppies to bird wings as soon as their eyes are open. They'll start to play tug-of-war with them, and I think it awakens that predator instinct in them. If you want them to be gundogs and work in the field, get them retrieving early. Start with small balls, paint rollers, or other objects. I like to practice in a closed hallway at first so they can't run off and escape with their prize.*
>
> **MARK LEE**
> *Holland Ridge Boykins*

If your Boykin Spaniel is getting a little too excited on the retrieve, as puppies often can, you may need to do a little extra work getting him to deliver to hand. Begin by walking your dog about twenty yards in the field and giving him the sit command. Give him the dummy and tell him to stay or hold. Walk back to your starting point, then recall the dog and tell him to heel. Practice this over and over. This practice eliminates the excitement of throwing the dummy and allows your Boykin to simply practice the delivery back to you.

Professional Training Facilities

If you are a serious hunter and plan to have your Boykin Spaniel by your side out in the field, you need to know that he understands what to do. This is important for the success of the hunt and also for the safety of the dog and the hunters. Sending your Boykin Spaniel to a professional

Photo Courtesy of John Gresko

training facility can be a huge benefit. While the cost and the time are significant factors, almost all who send their dogs away for training claim it is worth it for a life of obedience and success in the field.

While programs vary greatly across the United States, many basic hunting training programs are about two to three months in length. For more advanced or specific training, your dog may be required to stay at the training facility for four to six months. This may seem like a long time, and it is, but most choose to trade three to six months for a lifetime of obedience and pleasant dog ownership.

The cost is another big factor, as hunting dog training is not cheap. While the quality of the facility and location will cause the cost to vary, on average, training facilities cost over $1,000 a month, with the average required time being three months. If this is something you plan to seek for your Boykin Spaniel, plan ahead before you pick him up from the breeder. Ask your breeder, if they are local, about the best training facilities. They should be able to connect you with a reputable training facility that consistently puts out good dogs. Once you've found a facility, they will be able to talk to you about your specific Boykin Spaniel and let you know when they think he is ready for training.

Once your dog returns home, a good training facility will equip you with the knowledge and tools to continue your Boykin Spaniel's training. This is imperative to his and your success in the field, so do not neglect his continued training needs.

We really believe in the Bill Hillman technique of building a relationship with your dog, where you become the reward. His Training a Retriever Puppy with Bill Hillman program should be in every Boykin puppy owner's toolbox.

PATRICIA DOWNEY

Bayhill Boykins

CHAPTER 12

Traveling with Your Boykin Spaniel

If you plan to hunt with your Boykin Spaniel, you may foresee needing to travel with your dog. Or maybe you simply love to travel and wish to take your four-legged friend along with you wherever you go. Either way, this chapter will look at all the ins and outs of traveling with your Boykin Spaniel and prepare you with the knowledge to help you make the best decision for you and your dog.

Flying with Your Dog

Flying with your Boykin Spaniel will take significant planning beforehand. There are only so many pets allowed on each airplane (this varies by airline and size of the plane), so book your flight as early as possible to obtain a spot. In the past, airlines treated cargo animals just like any other luggage. Dogs were often left traumatized and sometimes even died because of uncontrolled temperatures, lack of water, etc. Luckily, today, airlines have implemented regulations to keep animals housed in the cargo area as safe and happy as possible.

A fully mature Boykin Spaniel will most likely not be allowed to fly in the passenger area of the plane but will be checked into the cargo area in a crate. Most airlines charge a fee for transporting animals. It is usually somewhere between $75 and $200 each way. If possible, get a direct flight for you and your dog.

If you're flying with a very young pup, you may be able to have him in the cabin with you on a flight. Typically, the weight limit for pets in the cabin is 20–25 pounds, but every airline's rules and regulations are a little different. Check with your preferred airline before making plans. If your puppy is able to fly as a carry-on, he will likely have to remain in an airline-approved crate that is able to fit under the seat, approximately 17.5 inches by 12 inches by 7.5 inches tall. This can be a hard- or soft-shell crate, but it should be sturdy and well-ventilated.

FUN FACT

South Carolina State Dog

In April 1984, the South Carolina Wildlife and Marine Resources Commission designated the Boykin Spaniel the official state dog. The same year, Governor Richard W. Riley established September 1 as Boykin Spaniel Day, which is still celebrated. However, it wasn't until 2009 that the AKC gave Boykin Spaniels full recognition.

According to the AKC, "The Federal Aviation Administration considers the pet-travel crate to be carry-on luggage, and it must be put through the carry-on luggage screening device—but your puppy does not. When you go through security, carry the pup in your arms and take him through the human screening process."

While you may want to take your sweet Boykin Spaniel with you wherever you go, flying isn't a fun thing for dogs and causes them stress. No matter how much airlines have worked to improve the process for animals, air travel will still be traumatizing for your dog and does carry a bit of risk.

Guidelines for flying animals vary greatly based on the airline, so be sure to check with your specific airline before traveling. Some require a certificate of veterinary inspection (CVI) before flying. Make sure you do thorough research on each airline and choose the one you think suits your needs best. Choosing the right airline can make or break your traveling experience.

When it comes to airline-approved kennels, regulations are constantly changing. Check your local airline for current recommendations on preferred kennels and read consumer reviews. Just know that choosing a proper kennel is crucial for his safety and protection on a flight.

According to American Airlines, a kennel must be rigid, made from metal, plastic, or wood, and with no damage or cracks evident. It must be well-ventilated on three or four sides, and it must have a metal door. Collapsible kennels are prohibited. Depending on the type of flight or plane, there may be size requirements for the kennel, so call your airline for specifics.

Most airlines will allow you to attach a bag of food that may be used in case of delay. Some even allow a drip water dispenser for your dog on the flight, so it's important you let your dog practice with one of these before the flight if he is unfamiliar.

Many airlines will also allow a small blanket or piece of clothing in the crate with your scent to bring your dog comfort. So, if this is an option, utilize it! Most airlines have banned crate pads, toys, bones, or treats, as well as newspaper, straw, or hay bedding. Most also do not allow any collar other than a flat collar, meaning muzzles, shock collars, and metal collars are prohibited. Sending medication with your dog is also not allowed. Because each airline is different, confirm with your specific airline before you plan.

Because your Boykin Spaniel will have to be checked in with the luggage, it would be wise to arrive as close to flight time as possible so he does not have a long wait without you. Take your dog out to potty just before you leave for the airport, as grass is often difficult to find once you enter the airport property. If you have the opportunity, allow your dog to relieve himself just before entering the building as well. It is also wise to withhold food and water for a few hours before traveling so that your dog does not become sick on the flight.

Other Methods of Transportation

If traveling from city to city, you may consider a train. Unfortunately, dogs over 20 pounds are not allowed on Amtrak, which means your mature Boykin Spaniel will not be accommodated. If you are traveling with a very young pup under 20 pounds, know that dogs are not allowed on trips over seven hours, including loading time. Also, availability is limited for pets, so book early.

The fee for traveling with your pup on Amtrak is $26—far cheaper than air travel. If you choose to travel by train, check the latest kennel regulations to make sure you are in compliance.

Most bus lines do not allow medium to large dogs to ride unless they are service dogs. However, all bus lines are different, so check with your local bus service to find out if they allow dogs.

Photo Courtesy of Andrew Cawthon

Hotel Stays and House Rentals

Before planning overnight travel with your Boykin Spaniel, make sure you have hotel arrangements ahead of time if needed. Not all hotels are pet friendly, and even those that claim to be may have breed and size restrictions. Before booking, call and check their pet policy and make sure they will allow your Boykin Spaniel to stay. Sometimes, a hotel booking website will list a hotel as "pet friendly," but this doesn't always mean your dog can stay with you, so call ahead and get the details so that there aren't any surprises when you arrive.

Another thing to consider when choosing a hotel is whether or not it has adequate outdoor space. Even some "pet-friendly" hotels aren't actually convenient for pets, as there is no space to walk your dog or let him do his business. Be sure to request a room on the ground floor so that you don't have to take the stairs or elevator every time your dog needs to go outside.

Some hotels reserve old, outdated rooms for pets, so call and check ahead of time to see if the pet rooms are different from the other rooms. Even if you don't anticipate using it, bring a kennel to the hotel in case you must leave your dog unattended. You never know when an emergency will happen, and it's better to be prepared.

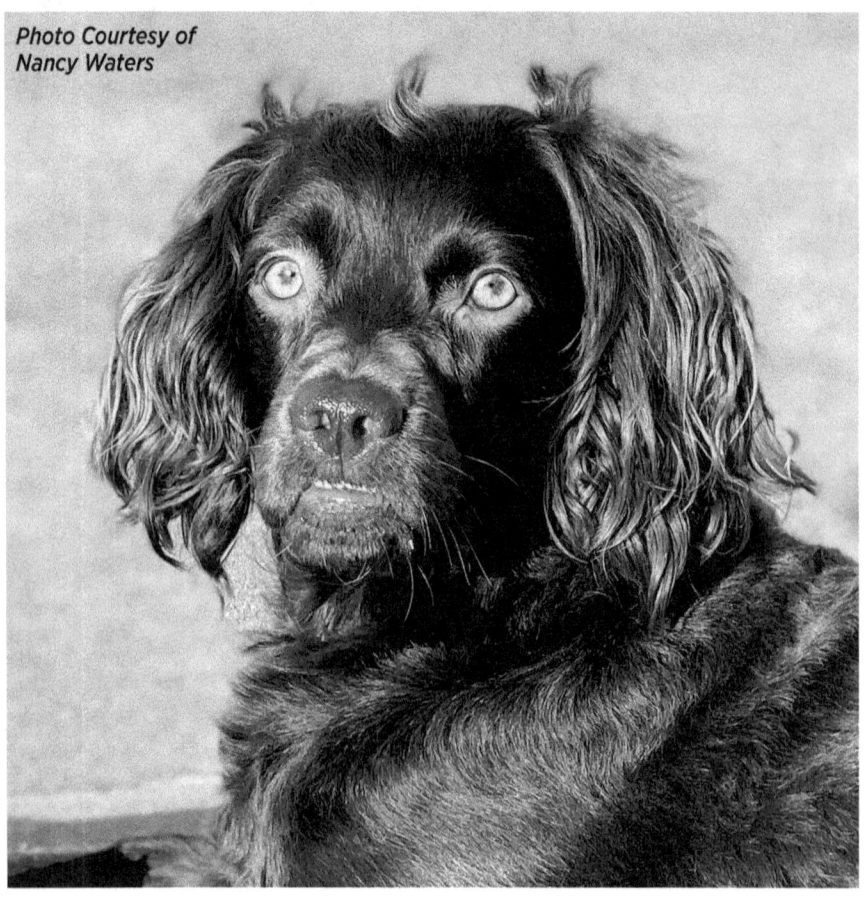

Photo Courtesy of Nancy Waters

These same principles apply to Airbnb and VRBO rentals as well. Double-check that a property is dog-friendly and has adequate accommodations and outdoor space before you book.

When to Leave Your Boykin Spaniel Behind

As we've discussed, traveling with your Boykin Spaniel may not be as simple as you wish. Often, it causes distress and puts your dog in less-than-ideal situations. Obviously, if you are traveling with your dog for a hunting trip, you will need to use the information given to determine the best mode of transportation. However, if you are simply traveling for fun and wish to take your Boykin Spaniel along for companionship, it may be wise to know when to leave him behind. There are several options for dog care while you're away that are not only safe but are sometimes downright fun for your dog!

Kenneling vs. Dog Sitting

There are two basic choices for care while you are gone. You can put your dog at a boarding kennel until you return, or you can hire a dog sitter. Depending on your needs and the personality of your dog, either of these can be a great option. You can also ask a family member or friend to care for your dog while you are away. Just be sure they are responsible and care for your Boykin Spaniel as much as you do!

If you won't be gone for an extended period, you might find hiring a dog sitter a more affordable option. This is typically when you hire someone to come and take your dog out two to three times a day and make sure he has food and water. You might hire a professional dog sitter or a trusted friend or family member. Because this breed requires so much exercise and companionship, this is only a good option for a day or two. After this, your dog may begin to feel cooped up and anxious, likely becoming destructive.

You can also hire a 24-hour dog sitter who will stay overnight to care for your dog. This will, of course, be a more expensive option. It will allow your dog to have companionship and constant care, however, which is something your dog will enjoy.

A boarding kennel is likely the best option for your Boykin Spaniel if he is well-socialized and gets along well with other dogs. Most of these places allow your dog to play with other dogs in a safe environment for most of the day. A stay at a boarding kennel can be like a vacation for your dog!

Every boarding facility is different and enforces its own unique rules and policies. The accommodations range from basic kennels to full-sized rooms with elevated dog beds and doggy doors to a private patio. Many even have cameras set up so you can check in on your dog from your phone.

Frequently, quality boarding facilities will have a common area inside and out where dogs can play and romp. The cost per night varies greatly depending on location and amenities.

Every quality kennel will require a Bordetella vaccine before your dog's stay. Never take your dog to a place that doesn't ask for this.

Photo Courtesy of
Sheila McMurry

Bordetella is highly contagious and common, and it only takes one dog to cause an outbreak. Plan for your dog to get the vaccine a minimum of two weeks before his stay.

Ask around among other dog owners and check reviews before you choose a place to take your dog while you're away. You don't want to take your Boykin Spaniel just anywhere. Be sure you can trust that they will provide adequate care and interaction so that you can spend your trip having fun and not worrying about your dog!

Bonus Tips and Tricks for Traveling

Traveling with your Boykin Spaniel can be fun and exciting, but it can also be stressful. Follow these tips to help any trip with your loyal companion be a stress-free one!

- Don't feed your dog within four hours of any trip. This includes car rides, plane rides, and any other method of transportation. This may help prevent you from having to clean up vomit.
- Exercise your Boykin Spaniel vigorously the day before and the day of your trip. Let him get as much energy out as he possibly can before being put into his crate.
- Don't sedate your dog! This once-common practice is no longer recommended by veterinarians. Sedating a dog can inhibit his ability to react in an emergency and is simply not good for his health.
- Check-in as late as possible at the airport so that your dog doesn't have to spend extra time waiting.
- If you are flying, make sure that your rental car or car service allows for dogs to ride.
- Always have a bowl, leash, water, and plastic waste bags with you. No matter how you are traveling, these basic items will be daily necessities. If you're driving, use a safety harness, as discussed earlier, and stop often to let your dog potty and drink water.
- Always have the number of a local emergency vet on hand. Emergencies can happen anywhere, so look up local animal hospitals before you travel—just in case!

CHAPTER 13

Grooming Your Boykin Spaniel

The Grooming Needs of a Boykin Spaniel

> "
> *Grooming really depends on the dog's coat. Our longer-haired, curly Boykin gets regular trims to keep her hair from getting too long. Our medium-length, wavy girl just needs trims during hunting season to reduce the number of seeds that stick to her coat. Our shorter-haired girl needs very little trimming.*
>
> **PATRICIA DOWNEY**
> *Bayhill Boykins*
> "

The wavy, rich-colored coat of the Boykin Spaniel is beautiful and low maintenance. According to the AKC, a weekly brush and an occasional bath will be enough to keep the coat clean and looking its best. There are some hunters who choose to give their Boykin Spaniels a field cut to help keep the body free of debris in the field. We'll discuss this special clip later in this chapter.

Photo Courtesy of
Edith Hines
Woodland Holler Boykins

Coat Basics

A Boykin Spaniel typically has a medium-length single coat, although some individuals may have an undercoat. Their coat is often wavy, with beautiful feathering on the ears, chest, legs, and belly. The Boykin Spaniel's coat is either a rich dark brown or liver color, providing natural protection for fieldwork. The presence of an undercoat in some individuals helps keep them warm and dry in harsh conditions, further enhancing their suitability as an outdoor companion.

Essential Grooming Tools

Even if you choose not to clip your Boykin Spaniel, you will need to have a few other grooming tools on hand for basic care. Invest in a quality pet brush, shampoo, and conditioner, and aim to bathe your dog once every month or two.

The choice of shampoo is based on your personal preference, so you may have to try a few out before finding one that is right for you and your dog. Whichever shampoo you choose, make sure it is free from parabens, dyes, sulfates, and DEA. These are ingredients commonly used in commercial shampoos but are known to have potentially damaging effects over time. It is also best to avoid any added fragrances, especially if your dog has sensitive skin.

Finding a grooming brush for your dog can easily become overwhelming because there are so many types of brushes, all created for different purposes and coat types. Since Boykin Spaniels have medium-length fur, they can be prone to tangles and mats. A slicker brush is ideal for removing mats and tangles, as it has short, fine wire bristles that are effective for this purpose. In addition to a slicker brush, a de-matting comb is highly recommended for dealing with more stubborn mats. You may also want to purchase a natural bristle brush as a finishing brush; these brushes have tightly packed bristles that help to stimulate the skin's natural oils, keeping your dog's coat shiny and healthy.

Aside from coat care, you will also need to have nail trimmers, styptic powder, a dog toothbrush, toothpaste, and ear wash.

Photo Courtesy of Reagan McColl

Bathing and Brushing

As mentioned before, regular brushing and occasional baths are the keys to keeping your Boykin Spaniel clean and his coat healthy. You shouldn't bathe your dog more than once a month as this can strip the oils from the skin and cause dryness.

It is good practice to use a blow dryer to blow any excess dirt or hair off your dog's coat before putting him in the bath. Keep the dryer far enough off the coat to avoid causing tangles. After this, proceed with shampooing your dog.

When shampooing your dog, use quality dog shampoo. If you are unsure of what to use, ask local vets and groomers what they recommend. Never use human shampoo or conditioner on your dog.

It is best to bathe your dog in a tub with a hand sprayer, but a large rinsing cup will do if necessary. Make sure you clean the coat all the way down to the skin. Rinse with cool water and then use a towel to blot dry. Don't use the towel to rub your dog dry because this will cause tangles and mats to form in the coat.

Finish with a hairdryer and use the bristle brush to remove any tangles. Once finished, check the consistency of the coat with your hands. If one area feels denser, go back over that area with the brush to remove any mats.

Nail Trimming

Some people choose to have a groomer or a veterinarian trim their dog's nails for them, but you can easily do this at home with the right tools. You will need to invest in a quality nail trimmer. There are several types to choose from, but they will all get the job done, so choose based on your preference and what is easiest for you to maneuver.

You should also purchase some styptic powder. This will stop any bleeding if you accidentally cut a nail too short. Most clippers will come with instructions on how to clip the nails, and it is important to follow them carefully to avoid injury to your dog.

If you wait until your dog is older to begin trimming his nails, he will likely be leery of the strange tool in your hand. Introduce the nail clippers to your Boykin Spaniel early and often, even if he doesn't need a nail trim, so he can become accustomed to the tool.

Let your dog explore and sniff the trimmers so he can

HELPFUL TIP
Wash and Wear Spaniels

Sometimes referred to as "wash and wear" spaniels, Boykins have a low-maintenance coat, requiring minimal trimming and brushing several times a week. However, these dogs are moderate shedders and may require additional brushing during high-shed times, such as fall and winter. In addition, Boykin Spaniels should never be shaved, as this could damage their insulated coat, which protects them from cold temperatures while swimming. You'll want several types of brushes for your Boykin's coat, including a slicker or pin brush for regular grooming and a metal comb for detangling knots.

feel comfortable with them. Practice holding them near his feet to show him that they are not a threat. Reward him with treats to create a positive association. This will lay the groundwork for easy nail trims in the future!

A dog's nail is made up of the nail and the quick. The quick is the pink part inside the nail. If your dog has light-colored nails, the quick may be visible, making it easier to avoid. If the nails are black, you will not be able to see the quick and will need to be extra cautious not to trim too far back. If you do hit the quick, this is called quicking and is a very painful experience for your dog. It will bleed a lot, so immediately apply styptic powder.

The two most common types of nail trimmers are the guillotine type and the scissor type. To use the guillotine or scissor trimmers, carefully place the dog's nail into the clipper and cut at a 45-degree angle away from the pad. Remember, the longer a dog's nails, the longer the blood supply is inside the nail, so only trim a little at a time, even if your dog's nails are overgrown. As the nail is trimmed shorter, the blood supply will also retreat, making it possible to shorten his nails over time. Trim a small amount every ten days or so until the nails are the length you want. If you cause bleeding, stop it immediately with styptic powder.

Cleaning the Eyes and Ears

> "
>
> *Boykins, like other Spaniels, are prone to ear infections and need to have their ears washed with a cleaner after any water activities. When sitting on the couch, you can flip the ears up so they can 'air out,' and that helps prevent the moisture from getting trapped.*
>
> **AUDRA BOYKIN**
> *Legacy Boykins*
>
> "

The Boykin Spaniel does not need specific eye care other than keeping the eyes clean and free of debris—however, this breed can be prone to ear infections. Weekly flushing is necessary to clean your dog's ears and get out trapped debris and waxy buildup. This is especially true for

Photo Courtesy of Kelly Graham

Boykin Spaniels who work in the field. To do this, gently squeeze the cleaning solution into one ear as directed on the bottle. Massage the ear canal and then move on to the other ear. You may need someone to help you hold your dog while you put the liquid in his ear.

Dental Care

> 66
>
> *For overall good health, start brushing your puppy's teeth immediately. Keep the nails trimmed regularly, and plan to brush the dog two to three times each week. If you start this when Boykins are puppies, they will not resist it as they get older.*
>
> TABBY LANGLEY
> *Tabby's Sweet Boykins*
> 99

Dental health is often overlooked when it comes to dogs, but proper oral care is important! Dogs can suffer from the same oral diseases and pain that humans do. Your dog should be taken to the vet every year or two for a professional dental cleaning. Talk to your vet about how often he or she recommends.

At home, brush your dog's teeth often with a dog-specific toothpaste to prevent any oral issues down the road. Never use human toothpaste, which is full of additives that are meant to be spat out and not swallowed. Brush gently and take it slow until your dog is accustomed to the toothbrush. If your dog is wary, begin by putting dog toothpaste on your finger and in your dog's mouth. Slowly work your way up to rubbing the toothbrush on his lips and eventually against his teeth. It is a good idea to do this at the same time you brush his coat every week to create a routine.

Brushing is not the only way to help your dog keep his teeth in tip-top shape. Chewing has been shown to naturally reduce plaque and tartar buildup. Dental chews come in many sizes, so just make sure you get the right size for your dog. When using these, it is advisable to have your dog on your lap and hold one end of the chew in your hand as he enjoys the chomping. This will ensure that your precious pup does not try to swallow a piece that is too big for him and might cause choking.

How to Clip at Home

> *Keep the inside of the ear hair cut down. The hair may grow too long and cause ear infections due to lack of airflow. The hair is there to keep stuff, such as seeds and pollen, from getting in, but it should not keep anything stuck in there either.*
>
> **JAMES ZILKA**
> *Muddy Creek Boykins*

Many suggest giving a Boykin Spaniel a "summer cut" to both keep the dog cooler and help the coat dry faster after being in the water, preventing any skin irritation or infection. This light grooming can easily be done with a basic grooming kit, including a comb and a pair of shears. Simply trim the fur all over your Boykin's body, being sure not to miss the underside of his ears and the fur that grows between his toes.

Clipping any dog at home is no easy job. If you plan to embark on the endeavor, arm yourself with the proper tools and setup to make the grooming session much easier for both you and your dog. If perfection is what you're after, consider having your Boykin Spaniel professionally groomed.

When to Seek Professional Help

> *When I go to my groomer, I tell them that I want a full trim. This helps eliminate some of the shedding. I also tell them to trim the back of the legs, the feet, and behind the ears and tail. I have not found a 'specific' cut, but I also enjoy the natural look of the Boykins. I highly suggest not shaving a Boykin, especially in the summer. Their coats naturally regulate as seasons pass (hence the shedding) to protect them.*
>
> JONATHON GRABARA
> *Tradewater Kennels*

If you want your Boykin Spaniel to sport that summer cut but aren't quite confident in your own grooming skills, take your dog to a professional groomer. They not only have experience that will produce a beautiful result, but they can also make the process easier for a nervous dog! Ask your vet or friends and family who have dogs for groomer references so that you're sure you choose a good one.

CHAPTER 14

Basic Health Care

Veterinary Care

> " There are many health issues associated with Boykin Spaniels. Getting a puppy from a reputable breeder is a good start to getting a healthy dog but is not a guarantee. Preventing blockages from ingesting inappropriate things is imperative and requires hypervigilance. Puppies are curious and will eat anything they think is interesting.
>
> **EDITH HINES**
> *Woodland Holler Boykins*
> "

Even in good health, your Boykin Spaniel should see the vet routinely for check-ups and vaccinations. These appointments typically happen yearly unless there is a reason to come in more frequently. At these yearly check-ups, the vet will give your dog a good look-over to make sure things are functioning properly. The vet should listen to your dog's heart and lungs and examine the ears, eyes, nose, and mouth. The visit should also include an abdominal examination, looking for any abnormalities. The vet may draw blood to check for heartworms and take a stool sample to check for other parasites. Sometimes, the vet will examine your dog's gait and coat condition.

Photo Courtesy of Kelly Graham

Boykin Spaniels, like most purebred dogs, are susceptible to a few genetic conditions. These annual visits with your vet may allow you to catch any issues early before they become worse.

Fleas and Ticks

Fleas are a common parasite that plague dogs, and they are a problem almost everywhere in the world. These tiny parasites reproduce quickly, with a female flea laying 20 to 40 eggs a day. This means a single flea in your home can quickly turn into an infestation that can be difficult to get rid of.

Ticks largely go unnoticed by their host, but they can cause a much bigger health problem than fleas, as they are notorious for transmitting dangerous diseases to dogs, humans, and other animals. Although ticks prefer a dog over a human, they will latch on to you if given the opportunity. For this reason, it is important to keep your dog protected from ticks at all times.

Flea and tick prevention are important for your dog's health and for your own. There are many options when it comes to prevention. Understanding the benefits and the disadvantages of each one will allow you to choose which is best for your dog.

Topical flea and tick preventative medication is common and easily accessible without a prescription. Typically, this medication comes in a small tube that the owner squeezes onto the dog's back between the shoulder blades. This topical medication usually takes about 12 hours to take effect and will last about 30 days before it needs to be reapplied. This works because the solution is absorbed into the skin and circulates through the dog's bloodstream, treating fleas and ticks over the entire body, not just the area it was directly applied.

One disadvantage of this application is it usually leaves a greasy spot on your dog's back for a few days. Considering this is a medication, it's not something you want to touch yourself or allow children to come in contact with. There is usually a minimum age requirement for these medications, so it is best to consult your vet before applying them to a young Boykin Spaniel pup.

Another method of administration is oral medication. There are numerous tablets on the market that prevent fleas and ticks for 30 days. Some of these prevent heartworms and internal parasites as well. Depending on how your dog takes medication, this could be an easier way to prevent the parasites without the mess of topical medication. Just as with any medication, side effects do exist. While they are generally mild, some dogs can react with skin irritations, vomiting, or diarrhea.

You can also buy a special flea collar for your dog. These are collars worn in addition to your dog's identification collar. They are covered with topical flea medications, usually permethrin. This provides up to eight months of protection for your dog but can also cause skin irritation. While these collars have been deemed safe for dogs, permethrin can cause toxicity in cats. Just like with topical medication, children and adults should avoid contact with the active ingredients on flea collars. As with topical medications, flea collars should never be used on a young puppy, and the same precautions should be taken.

Even a dog that lives primarily indoors should be on a flea and tick preventative. It only takes one exposure to one of these parasites to potentially spell bad news for you and your dog. It is much better to take preventative measures than to have to deal with fleas or ticks after they have hitched a ride into your home.

If you suspect your dog might have fleas, you can purchase a flea comb at any pet store. Flea combs have very fine and closely spaced teeth that fleas cannot pass between. Run the flea comb over your dog's body at a 45-degree angle, focusing on the head, neck, and hindquarters, where fleas often congregate. If you see a flea in the comb, cover it quickly and trap it in a wet paper towel. Drop the flea in a bowl of soapy water to kill it.

Photo Courtesy of
Hanna Brown

You may give your dog a flea bath with a medicated shampoo, but mild dish soap is also proven effective at killing adult fleas without the harmful ingredients in a flea shampoo. Flea baths are only effective at killing adult fleas and are ineffective at killing larvae and eggs. This means they are a temporary solution, and as the larvae mature and the eggs hatch, the fleas will reappear on your Boykin Spaniel.

Once you have addressed the fleas on your dog, shift the focus to your home, as there may be fleas lurking there as well, waiting to rein-fest your dog. Vacuum your entire house from the floor to the curtains. Anything upholstered is potentially a place where a flea has laid eggs. If you notice fleas in your home, continue vacuuming twice a day for two weeks in order to get rid of all the fleas as they hatch. Fleas reproduce quickly, so don't skip a day!

Tick-Related Illnesses

Lyme Disease – This common tick-borne disease carries serious risks for both humans and dogs. Transmitted by the black-legged tick, also called the deer tick, this disease is present across the United States, but it is more prevalent in the Northeast.

Lyme Disease in dogs presents much like it does in humans, with flu-like symptoms, such as fever, chills, aches, and swollen lymph nodes. These signs can be difficult to detect in dogs, so watch for any change in behavior, apparent discomfort, or loss of appetite. If caught early, Lyme Disease can typically be treated successfully with an antibiotic, but prompt treatment is a must, so do not delay treatment.

If your vet suspects Lyme Disease, he will perform a C6 test to detect antibodies. This disease cannot be passed from an infected dog to a human or another dog. It can only be transmitted via tick bite.

Anaplasma – Symptoms of anaplasma are similar to Lyme Disease but also include low platelets, usually evident by unusual bleeding or bruising. This disease is typically found in the Northeast United States, the upper Midwest, and the Western Coastal states.

Canine Ehrlichiosis – This tick-borne illness is found all over the world. Symptoms include loss of appetite, low platelets, and fever. If you notice your Boykin Spaniel is unwell after a tick bite, take him to the vet promptly to avoid chronic symptoms that are difficult to manage.

Rocky Mountain Spotted Fever – This is another common tick-borne disease that affects both humans and animals. It is typically found in ticks around the United States and in Central and South America. Symptoms of Rocky Mountain Fever are similar to others and include fever, loss of appetite, joint pain, low platelets, swollen lymph nodes, and occasionally neurological signs.

Babesiosis – Babesiosis can cause hemolysis, a breakdown of red blood cells, causing symptoms like jaundice, pale gums, dark urine, lethargy, depression, and sometimes, enlargement of the spleen. This disease can be fatal, so seek care for your dog immediately.

Tick Removal

Ticks and fleas are often treated using the same medication, as discussed in the previous section. Make sure your dog's preventative covers both fleas and ticks to help your Boykin Spaniel avoid serious infection and disease.

Preventative medication is especially important if your dog goes on hunts with you in wooded areas or areas with tall brush. If your dog does go through brush or tall grass, inspect him promptly when you get home and remove any ticks you find with the following steps.

1. With gloves on, use tweezers to grab the tick firmly and as close to the skin as possible.
2. Once you securely have the tick, pull straight up so none of the tick's mouthparts are left behind, causing infection.
3. Put the tick in a jar of soapy water to kill it, and clean the tick bite area thoroughly with antiseptic.
4. Keep the tick for identification purposes in the event your dog begins showing symptoms. These may take up to two weeks to present, so watch your dog closely for changing behavior.

Though both ticks and fleas can be seasonal in many regions, most vets recommend keeping your dog on a year-round preventative. Ticks can often go unnoticed by their host, but they pose a significant health risk to both you and your dog.

Worms and Other Parasites

Worms and parasites are common in dogs, but they can become harmful if left untreated. Common worms and parasites include hookworms, ringworm, roundworms, tapeworms, whipworms, coccidia, giardia, and spirochetes. These parasites are typically diagnosed via a stool sample, but there are some signs and symptoms you can watch for as well.

Photo Courtesy of
Jessica Burchette

Hookworm – Hookworm larvae live in the soil and can be picked up through common activities, such as walking through a park. These worms attach themselves to the intestinal walls and feed off your dog's blood. Diarrhea and weight loss are possible signs of hookworms.

Once your vet confirms a diagnosis, oral medication can be used to treat the parasite. Depending on the severity of the infestation, iron supplements may be needed to treat anemia. Young puppies are most susceptible to hookworms, as is the case with most parasites.

Ringworm – This is actually a fungus and not a worm. Ringworm causes circular bald patches on your dog's skin and is easily spread from dog to dog and even dog to human in some cases. Your vet will probably treat your dog with a medicated shampoo and an oral medication.

Roundworm – Roundworms are common and typically discovered when the owner spots round white worms in a dog's stool. These worms are typically an inch or two in length. Other symptoms of roundworm include coughing, vomiting, and diarrhea; however, these only present in severe cases. Ringworms can also be passed to humans, especially kids.

Tapeworm – Tapeworm is commonly caused by ingesting larvae, typically by eating a flea. Weight loss and diarrhea are common symptoms, as well as small worm segments in your dog's stool. These often resemble grains of rice. Treatment includes an oral medication and possible injections.

Whipworm – Whipworms live in the large intestine and are difficult to spot in a stool sample. Signs of infection may include a mucus covering at the tip of your dog's stool. These parasites are typically not serious but can cause weight loss. Treatment includes oral medication.

Coccidia, Giardia, and Spirochetes – These are not worms; they are single-celled parasites that can do much damage to your dog before you even know he is infected. These parasites can cause lasting diseases and issues for a dog and require swift treatment from a vet. Often transmitted through water, food, soil, and feces, these parasites live in unsanitary conditions.

Photo Courtesy of
Curtis Hooks
Blackwater - Kiona Rose

Young puppies and older dogs are more susceptible due to their weakened immune systems. Oral medication is needed.

Heartworm – Heartworms are much more severe than other intestinal parasites. These worms are transmitted via mosquito bite and typically take anywhere from six to seven months to develop into adult heartworms, which live in your dog's heart and cause major issues. These worms can cause lung, heart, and artery damage that may be permanent.

Treatment at the earliest signs of infection is crucial and may be the difference between life and death for your dog. Early symptoms include loss of appetite, cough, fatigue, and no motivation to get moving or play. As the disease progresses, these symptoms will become more severe and include bloating and even heart failure.

Heartworms are common in the southern portion of the United States, especially around the Gulf of Mexico; however, cases have been recorded in all 50 states. Preventative medication should be started around the age of six months. Options for this preventative include topical, oral, and injection. Discuss a detailed prevention plan with your vet.

Your vet will most likely require yearly heartworm testing for your Boykin Spaniel, even if he is on a preventative. Heartworm is very dangerous and difficult to treat. If your dog is diagnosed with heartworm disease, treatment can cost anywhere from $500 to $1,500 or more, and it isn't guaranteed to work.

Vaccinations

Vaccinations are an important tool for keeping your Boykin Spaniel healthy and safe from potentially life-threatening illnesses. These vaccines work by injecting the body with antigens to elicit an immune response, producing antibodies for those diseases. While your dog does not actually contract the disease after injection, the antibodies are able to build immunity to the disease going forward.

Distemper, adenovirus, hepatitis, parvovirus, and parainfluenza are considered the core vaccinations that every puppy should receive when nursing ends at about six weeks of age. These shots are usually given in 3 to 4 rounds: once at six weeks, 10 weeks, 14 weeks, and 18 weeks. Many vets prefer to administer these vaccines in one shot, called a 5-Way. Depending on where you live and your dog's risk factors, your vet may also recommend vaccinations for Bordetella and Leptospirosis.

The rabies vaccine is legally required in most areas and is administered separately, no sooner than 12 weeks of age. This vaccine must be administered every one to three years.

While these vaccines are mostly safe and effective, negative reactions can occur. Allergic reactions to vaccinations can cause hives, swelling, vomiting, and fever. Notify your vet immediately of any negative reactions, even if mild. The symptoms could worsen after the next round of shots.

Oftentimes, but not always, vaccinations are required to access many dog-related facilities. These may include kennels for boarding or daycare, groomers, and, sometimes, training facilities. Be sure to keep access to vaccination records in case you need to show proof.

Common Allergens

> "
>
> *Environmental allergies can cause itching and even hair loss. Watch for symptoms like excessive scratching and licking their feet.*
>
> DIANE WEBER
> *Webers Boykin Spaniels*
>
> "

Some Boykin Spaniels can have allergies, much like humans can. These may be allergies to foods or things in the environment. Depending on the allergen, your Boykin Spaniel may show signs of skin problems and itching. If your Boykin seems to have skin itchiness, try switching up his food. If that doesn't work and you suspect your dog may have allergies, discuss options for treatment with your vet.

Common Diseases and Conditions

Boykin Spaniels are relatively healthy purebred dogs. Even so, there are a handful of genetic conditions and common diseases this breed can develop. They are as follows:

Exercise-induced Collapse (EIC) – This inherited neuromuscular disease is characterized by an intolerance to significant or strenuous exercise. Boykin Spaniels afflicted by EIC may lose control of their limbs after a short burst of intense exercise, such as vigorously chasing a ball or participating in fieldwork. Most dogs recover within 30 minutes of collapse, but some do not. This disease can be fatal. Always ask a breeder if they test for EIC before purchasing a Boykin Spaniel puppy.

Degenerative Myelopathy – This degenerative disease is a genetic mutation known to be carried by some Boykin Spaniels. This disease causes a degeneration of the nerves in the spinal cord, causing progressive weakness and eventual paralysis in the hind legs. This disease is painless but debilitating for a Boykin Spaniel, and it typically begins in mid to late life.

Pulmonic Stenosis – This congenital heart defect is a narrowing between the right ventricle and the pulmonary artery. This can range in severity, with mild cases likely being mostly asymptomatic. More severe cases, however, may cause collapse, trouble exercising, and even heart failure.

According to PetMD, "Pulmonic stenosis results in increased pressure in the right side of the heart, which can lead to thickening of the heart muscle, heart failure, arrhythmias, and even sudden death. Puppies with pulmonic stenosis often have other congenital heart defects such as aortic stenosis and ventricular septal defect."

HEALTH ALERT
Health Testing for Boykin Spaniels

Boykin Spaniels are a generally healthy breed with limited health issues. The AKC recommends the following health testing:
- Hip Evaluation
- Patella Evaluation
- Exercise-Induced Collapse (EIC) DNA Test
- Ophthalmologist Evaluation
- Collie Eye Anomaly (CEA, CH) DNA Test

Hip Dysplasia – Hip dysplasia is a common inherited disease. This is when the hip joints fail to develop properly, which can lead to painful rubbing, arthritis, and even lameness. If you notice your dog moving painfully or getting up more slowly than usual, have him checked for dysplasia. Typically, the sooner it is caught, the more successful treatment is.

Usually not diagnosed until two years of age, hip dysplasia is not a life-threatening disease, but it can greatly reduce the quality of a dog's life. Sometimes, hip dysplasia can be managed with drugs, weight control, and monitored exercise. X-rays can determine the severity of the dysplasia. In severe situations, surgery may be the best option to give your Boykin Spaniel the fullest life possible.

NOTE:

Genetic testing is an essential part of responsible breeding for Boykin Spaniels, allowing breeders and owners to detect potential breed-specific disorders before breeding. The Boykin Spaniel Society recommends using Animal Genetics (https:// animalgenetics.com/), which offers discounted genetic testing panels for members, including tests for disorders like exercise-induced collapse (EIC), degenerative myelopathy (DM), and collie eye anomaly (CEA). This testing helps breeders ensure best practices for healthy litters and can also provide valuable information for non-breeding owners to monitor their dog's health. Members interested in genetic testing can contact the Boykin Spaniel Society for discount codes, one of the many benefits of membership.

Prevention

Genetic testing is the best method of prevention for serious conditions and diseases such as those mentioned above. This goes back to the importance of finding a reputable breeder who is dedicated to breeding only the best and healthiest Boykin Spaniels. Refer to Chapter 2 for tips on what to look for in a good breeder.

Holistic Alternatives and Supplements

Whether you are looking for a way to treat a sick Boykin Spaniel or you're just seeking preventative care, a healthy dog begins with a healthy lifestyle. This includes proper diet and exercise. Holistic alternatives are also becoming more and more common. These alternatives have been used for centuries and are getting some attention back in the spotlight as of late.

Acupuncture

Acupuncture involves pricking the skin with needles. It has notable benefits for managing pain and increasing circulation. Supporting overall wellness, acupuncture can aid in the treatment of hip dysplasia, allergies, gastrointestinal problems, and pain due to cancer treatments.

Acupuncture causes no pain and is shown to have a calming effect in pets. Though this is a promising alternative to medications, you should always consult your veterinarian before beginning any treatment. Acupuncture should only be performed by a certified acupuncturist.

Herbs

Not all herbs are safe for your dog. Some can interact with medications your dog may be taking and have unintentional ill effects. Discuss all herbs with your vet before adding them to your dog's diet or lifestyle. Some commonly used herbs include:

Goldenseal – Anti-inflammatory and antibacterial, goldenseal can be used externally on bodily infections or as an eyewash for infections or conjunctivitis. It can be taken internally at the first sign of kennel cough or digestive issues and can also be beneficial in the treatment of tapeworms and giardia. Goldenseal should not be used for too long as it can cause stress on the liver.

Milk Thistle – Milk thistle may protect against liver damage. If your dog is on any medication that can damage his liver, discuss adding milk thistle to his regimen with your vet.

Ginger – Just as with people, ginger is an effective tool for treating nausea and cardiovascular conditions in dogs. Ginger has cardiotonic effects and can promote the functionality of the heart.

Chamomile – Another herb that aids digestion, relieves muscle spasms, and reduces inflammation, chamomile is a great option for treating chronic bowel and gas disorders and can also ease your dog's anxiety.

HELPFUL TIP
Boykin Spaniel Club and Breeders Association of America (BSCBAA)

The Boykin Spaniel Club and Breeders Association of America (BSCBAA) is an organization dedicated to promoting and preserving the Boykin Spaniel breed. Founded in 1997, the BSCBAA is this breed's official American Kennel Club (AKC) parent club. The primary function of this club is to maintain the integrity and health of the Boykin Spaniel by upholding a breed standard that prioritizes these dogs' health, temperament, and abilities. In addition to these goals, the BSCBAA provides information and education about this breed and organizes annual events. For more information about the BSCBAA, visit https://boykinspanielclub.us/.

Licorice – Licorice root is a fast-acting anti-inflammatory that can be used to treat arthritis and other inflammatory diseases. It has been shown to enhance the efficacy of other herbs, so it is often combined with others as a part of a treatment plan.

CBD

The AKC's website states, "Currently, there has been no formal study on how CBD affects dogs. What scientists do know is that cannabinoids interact with the endocannabinoid receptors located in the central and peripheral nervous systems, which help maintain balance in the body and keep it in a normal healthy state."

CBD oil, also known as cannabidiol, is thought to treat pain and help control seizures in dogs. Anecdotal evidence also shows that CBD oil may have anti-inflammatory, anti-cancer, anti-anxiety, and cardiac benefits. Discuss with your vet the option of adding a CBD supplement to your dog's diet.

This is not a comprehensive list of herbs used for dogs. If you want your dog to experience the benefits of herbal remedies but can't source the herbs yourself, there are many premade solutions and tinctures available, conveniently packaged and mixed with directions. This can help ensure you are using the herb correctly.

Only use herbs and supplements from reputable and trustworthy companies. Beware of cheaper products that may contain synthetics. Always consult your vet before beginning any herbal treatment for your Boykin Spaniel.

Pet Insurance

> "
>
> *Purchase pet insurance. There are a variety of companies that provide pet insurance, and I don't have a recommendation on any specific one—just pick one. It will be the best investment you can make. It should be the first thing you do when you decide on a puppy. Purchase pet insurance first, and second, take them to the vet for a meet and greet and check-up. Pet insurance is a must!*
>
> DAWN CRITES
> *Lily Pad Spaniels*
>
> "

Pet insurance is an option for your dog if you choose; however, this option needs to be carefully researched. While pet insurance can protect you in the event any conditions arise, it can also be costly. Each company offers different coverage, so be sure to read the fine print and understand any exclusions; there is almost always an annual deductible you must meet before insurance will cover any costs. Even after that is met, many policies only cover 80%, with wellness exams and vaccines not included.

Rates will depend on your dog's age and condition. Unless something considerable comes up, it may be more affordable to simply pay out of pocket for services. Ask your vet what pet insurance he recommends, and go from there.

CHAPTER 15

Proper Nutrition

> 66
>
> *Ask your breeder what they have been feeding and continue on that for several weeks. If you want to change your pup's diet, do so slowly by adding a bit of the new food at first and then increasing the amount over time. Frequent change is difficult on a dog's stomach, so find a good quality dry kibble and stick with it.*
>
> BILL CRITES
> *Boykin Spaniel Society Hunt Test Chairman*
>
> 99

Why Quality Food Matters

As humans, we know that what we eat matters. It makes a difference in how we feel, how well our bodies perform, and even how we look. For the sake of our health, we do our best to eat a balanced diet and avoid processed foods with harmful additives. These same rules apply when it comes to feeding our dogs. Just like humans, dogs need a certain balance of protein, fats, carbohydrates, vitamins, and minerals to keep their bodies going.

All commercial dog foods have been tested rigorously and are required to meet minimum nutritional requirements. That said, minimum requirements are not what is best for your dog's long-term health. Feeding your Boykin Spaniel low-quality dog food is the equivalent of feeding him junk food. Choosing a dog food that is made with the best ingredients and does not include preservatives and additives will help your dog function at his optimal level, potentially protecting against disease.

According to Dr. Hugh Stevenson, a veterinarian in Ontario, Canada, symptoms of poor nutrition include a dull, thin coat, poor-quality footpads (which can crack or bleed), weight problems, excess stool and gas, and passing undigested grain particles in feces. Quality dog nutrition leads to a lustrous coat, healthy skin and weight, and less stool due to more of the food being digestible. For the sake of your Boykin Spaniel, choose the highest quality food you have available to you, as this will be of immense benefit for years to come. Below, we will discuss different dog food options you may consider for your dog.

Photo Courtesy of Tammy Duke

Types of Commercial Dog Foods

> ❝
>
> *As long as you are supplying very good quality kibble, don't worry if your puppy appears to be slightly on the thin side if he is bright and active. That is actually healthier for growing bones and joints. It's normal for a Boykin to take two years or more to mature to the ideal adult weight.*
>
> **PATRICIA DOWNEY**
> *Bayhill Boykins*
>
> ❞

There are many dog foods that claim to be the best, healthiest, and most complete. It can be both overwhelming and confusing. Should you buy dry kibble? Canned wet food? Each contains a different list of ingredients and promises on the label. So, how do you really know what you're getting?

The first choice you will have to make is whether to feed your dog dry kibble or wet food. Each choice comes with its own set of positives and negatives.

Wet Dog Food – Wet dog food has a very strong smell. This may be a positive for a dog who is particularly picky or doesn't have much interest in eating, as the strong scent may entice him to eat. It could also be a negative if you don't want to smell the food in your home every time you feed your dog. Wet food also helps with hydration if you have a dog that doesn't drink as much as he should, but it spoils quickly after opening. If your dog doesn't finish his food promptly, you'll need to store the rest in the refrigerator. Canned food can also be a bit messier to eat, getting caught in a Boykin Spaniel's chin and ears.

Dry Dog Food – Dry dog food doesn't spoil when left out. This is beneficial for a dog who may like to come back to his food and finish later. Dry dog food also doesn't have much of a smell, so it can sit out without anyone noticing. Some dry kibble is formulated to help clean your dog's teeth while he chews, although some experts say the added grains in certain dry foods contribute to tooth decay.

Whichever type of food you choose for your dog, it's important to remember that both canned food and kibble exist in low-quality forms. Low-quality brands include cheap fillers, artificial colors, flavors, and preservatives and should be avoided.

Ingredients to Avoid

It can be confusing reading the ingredient list on a dog food label. Companies that produce low-quality dog food use vague terms and scientific words to try and make you think the product contains quality, wholesome ingredients when it may not. Below is a list of key ingredients to avoid when searching for the best commercial dog food for your Boykin Spaniel.

BHA/BHT – Studies are not conclusive, but these chemical preservatives have been linked to hyperactivity and cancer. Used to preserve fats in human food and pet food, BHA and BHT have been banned in some countries but are still allowed in the United States, Canada, and Europe. Until conclusive evidence proves these preservatives are safe, it's best to avoid them altogether.

Meat, Meat Meal, or Rendered Fat – Any time you see a vague, nonspecific term such as "meat" or "meat meal," you can bet these are the lowest-quality ingredients allowed. These ingredients are leftovers from slaughterhouses—the parts humans won't eat. It can also include leftover, expired meats from the grocery store and diseased or dying livestock. Instead, look for specific meat terms you recognize, such as turkey, beef, salmon, lamb, or chicken.

If your dog food contains salmon or salmon meal, make sure it's labeled "wild-caught." Farm-raised salmon is less nutrient-dense than its wild counterpart because of the unnatural diet the fish are fed and has been found to potentially contain more contaminants.

Nitrites and Nitrates – Nitrites and nitrates, chemical additives used to preserve freshness and extend the shelf life of meat products, are found in human and dog food. Sodium nitrite can be toxic to your dog in high doses and has been linked to cancer.

Soy – Soy is cheap and readily available. Dog food manufacturers may use it as an inexpensive way to boost the protein percentage of the food, but it can be difficult for your dog to digest and can cause gastrointestinal upset.

Other ingredients to avoid include meat by-products, sodium hexametaphosphate, food dyes, carrageenan, taurine, cellulose, artificial flavors, and corn syrup. Dog food manufacturers dedicated to producing a quality, superior dog food will not use these red-flag ingredients. Though they can be a bit more expensive, the cost will be well worth it and may even save you money in vet bills in the long term by nourishing your dog properly.

HELPFUL TIP
Protein Consumption

Boykin Spaniels are high-energy dogs with moderate exercise needs. Therefore, your dog's protein intake should be tailored to his activity level. For example, some experts suggest that highly active dogs who regularly partake in hours of exercise or hunting should eat a diet with about 22 to 25% protein, while less active dogs may need only 18% protein. Any dietary changes should be discussed with your veterinarian before implementation.

There has been a recent trend in grain-free dog food. Some claim that because wolves in the wild don't consume more than a trace amount of grains, domesticated dogs shouldn't either. The truth is that dogs are not genetically identical to wolves, and they have adapted to utilize grains effectively.

Grain-free dog food contains other plants instead of grains. These are usually peas, lentils, potatoes, and legumes. These plant sources provide the starch to make the kibble and supply an added protein boost, allowing the manufacturer to cut back on the more expensive animal proteins. This can lead to a depletion of the amino acid taurine. Taurine is found in animal proteins but not in plant proteins, and the FDA has linked a lack of taurine to a rise in cardiomyopathy in dogs who have been fed a grain-free diet. It is best to discuss with your vet what food is best for your dog before jumping on the grain-free trend.

Homemade Dog Foods

The only way to know exactly what your Boykin Spaniel is eating is to take matters into your own hands and prepare homemade dog food. If you have the time and the resources to do this, homemade dog food can be a wonderful source of balanced whole foods for your dog, providing him with optimal nutrition without the fillers and preservatives present in commercial foods. In addition, food cooked at home contains more nutrients than processed food. This is because the high temperature used during processing causes a significant loss of nutrients.

Many homemade dog food recipes can be found online, but it's very important that you discuss specific recipes with your vet to be sure they provide your dog with all the nutrients he needs. Individual breeds and even dogs of the same breed can have different nutritional needs. When making your dog's food yourself, it's important to get a professional opinion regarding ingredients and serving size.

Table Food – What Is Good and What Is Bad?

> *Our Boykins love snacks of raw carrot sticks, sweet potato, sweet bell pepper slices, and even small amounts of raw broccoli, cauliflower, and cabbage.*
>
> PATRICIA DOWNEY
> *Bayhill Boykins*

If you want to feed your Boykin Spaniel scraps from the table, it is important you know what he can and cannot have off your plate. In Chapter 3, we covered a list of foods that would be dangerous for your dog to eat. You may want to refresh your memory before reading this list of foods that are okay for your dog to eat.

Remember, feeding your dog directly from the table can quickly form bad habits such as begging. This may be cute the first time, but it can get old fast when you want to enjoy a meal in peace.

There are several things you can safely share with your dog from your kitchen as a special treat or snack, but remember that these should be given in moderation so that they don't upset the balance of your dog's nutrition. None of these items should be heavily seasoned, as this may cause an upset stomach.

- White and brown rice
- Cooked eggs
- Oatmeal
- Carrots
- Cheese
- Peanut butter (without xylitol)
- Berries
- Green beans
- Seedless watermelon
- Bananas
- Peas
- Pineapple
- Apples
- Broccoli
- Potatoes

This is not a comprehensive list, and food sensitivities can differ from dog to dog, so consult your veterinarian if you think your dog may have a food allergy or sensitivity.

Weight Management

Keep Boykins healthy and in shape and they will live longer and healthier lives. Many dogs that we see are far overweight; thus 'in-shape' dogs look 'too skinny.' No fine-tuned athlete is overweight or out of shape—neither should our dogs be!

JONATHON GRABARA
Tradewater Kennels

An overweight dog can have significant health issues. In fact, just being overweight can significantly impact his quality of life in the short term, especially as he ages. Both diet and exercise should be evaluated to see where the problem may be originating.

Begin by implementing a more active routine. Your Boykin Spaniel requires much physical activity and should be engaging in a significant amount every single day. If he is not, his weight may suffer. Consult

Chapter 9 for ideas to make exercise fun for you and your dog. If your Boykin Spaniel has not been exercising, ease him into a regular routine and increase the intensity as his body allows.

Also, consider where your dog is getting his nutrition. Is he eating a quality commercial food? Low-quality foods contain filler ingredients that will fill your dog up temporarily but don't provide adequate nutrients. Your dog may end up eating more of these foods to make up for the lack of nutrition, causing weight issues. If you prepare homemade dog food for your pup, you may need to go back to the vet or nutritionist to reevaluate ingredients and portion sizes.

Is your dog eating too many snacks outside mealtime? You may love sharing a snack or two throughout the day, but if it is negatively impacting his weight and health, you should keep the snacking to a minimum. Remember, moderation is key.

If you can't get your dog's weight under control by limiting snacks and providing a quality commercial food, discuss options with your vet. He or she may suggest a weight management food. These foods feature higher than average protein, lower than average fat, and fewer calories. These foods are formulated for adult dogs only and should never be given to a puppy. Remember to read food labels and choose a food made with high-quality ingredients.

CHAPTER 16

Dealing with Unwanted Behaviors

> " The puppy stage can last a long time. I've had puppies that would chew and destroy things till they were two years old. Don't set the puppy up for failure. Don't leave it in situations where it can get into trouble. If it is not being supervised, crate or confine the animal. It's not being cruel to the dog. At later stages of life, the dog can have more freedom, but not when it is a puppy.
>
> MARK LEE
>
> *Holland Ridge Boykins* "

What Is Considered Bad Behavior?

We all know that dogs have personalities as unique as humans. Even within the same breed, no two dogs will be alike! Everyone wants a well-trained, obedient dog that will sit quietly waiting for the next command, but even successful training won't keep a spunky dog from being spunky. Just like humans, dogs can exhibit behaviors that are annoying at times, but that doesn't necessarily mean they are bad. So, when it comes to bad habits and behaviors, what is considered "bad?"

Barking – Barking is as natural for your dog as speaking is to you and should never be considered bad behavior. If your dog is extra chatty and

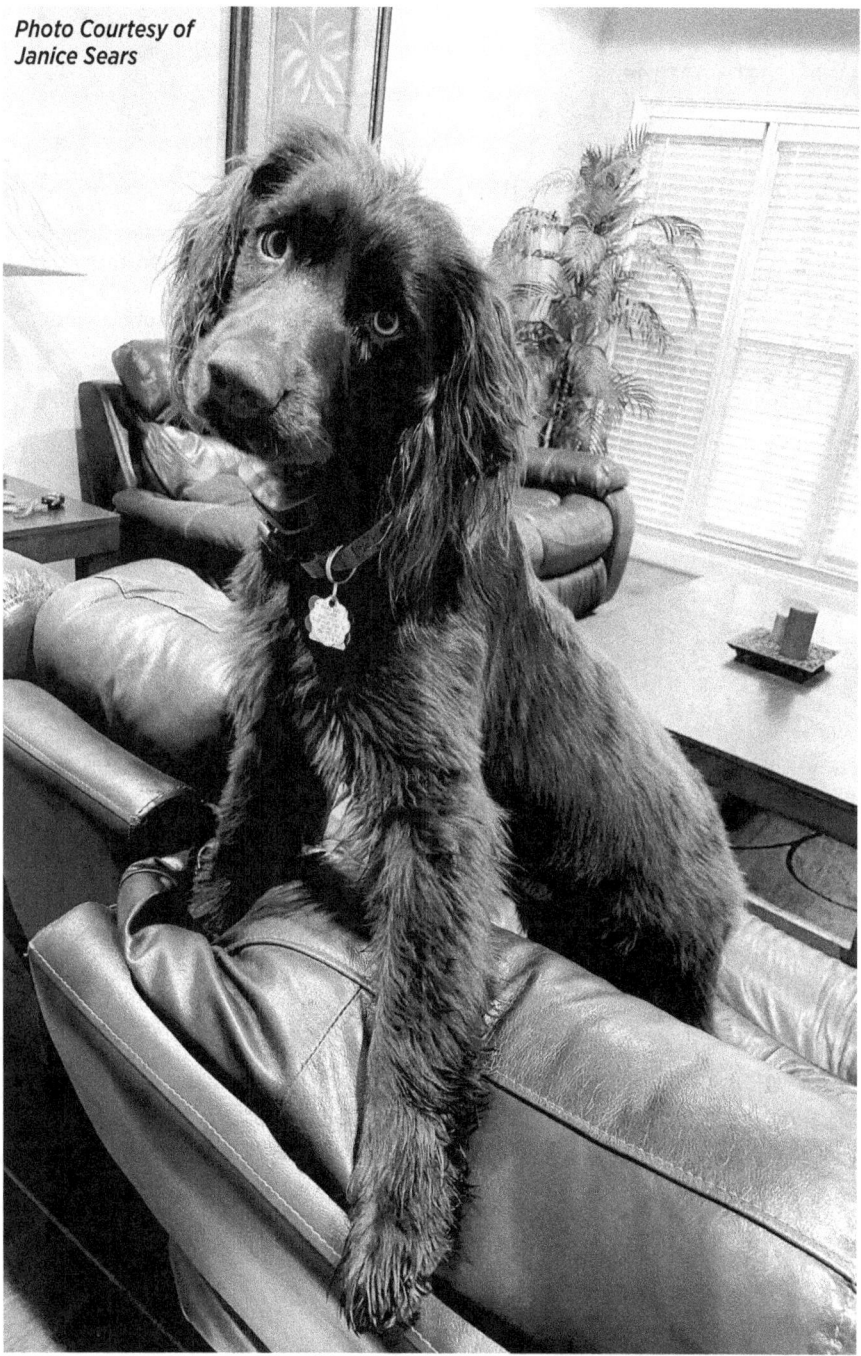

Photo Courtesy of Janice Sears

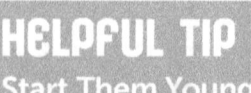

you find this to be an annoy-ance, there are measures you can take to correct the behavior.

First, determine if there is a reason for the behavior. Is there a direct cause for the barking, such as your Boykin Spaniel seeing other people or dogs? If so, socializing your dog may go a long way to stop the behavior.

If the problem is more sporadic and inconsistent, consider whether your dog may simply be trying to get your attention. Are you spending enough

HELPFUL TIP
Start Them Young

Early and frequent socialization is one of the best preventative measures against future behavior issues for your Boykin Spaniel. By exposing your dog to various environments, people, and other animals from a young age, you can help him develop into a well-rounded and well-behaved adult dog. Remember that Boykin Spaniels thrive on positive reinforcement and reward-based training methods when responding to unwanted behaviors.

intentional time with your dog? Is he getting enough social and physical engagement throughout the day? Barking may be your Boykin Spaniel's method of getting attention.

Digging – Much like chasing, digging is a natural behavior and may involve rolling around in the freshly disturbed dirt. This is not bad behavior. But it can become annoying and may be curbed with stricter supervision and obedience training.

Chasing – While this can be annoying and dangerous, it should never be treated as "bad" behavior. Your dog is only doing what comes naturally to him. Obedience training can help the issue, but it may not ever stop it completely.

Though not bad behavior, chasing can be a dangerous habit, especially in a city with cars and other hidden dangers. Unless you can be sure he won't chase a neighborhood cat or a skateboarder riding down the street, you will need to keep your dog leashed or contained behind a fence the entire time he is out.

Leash Pulling – This is a direct result of improper or inadequate training and is not bad behavior. Teach your dog the proper way to

*Photo Courtesy of
Michelle Hansen*

walk on a leash with the help of a trainer, and this annoyance can be eliminated altogether.

Other unwanted behaviors that are not "bad" include chewing up toys or shoes, begging or stealing food, jumping on people, getting on furniture, and eating poop. All of these behaviors can be a nuisance but are typically not evidence of a poorly behaved dog.

Aggression – Behavior that should always be considered "bad" is any form of unprovoked aggression. This includes food or possession aggression. It could be

Photo Courtesy of Tammy Duke

vicious growling, biting, lunging, or snarling. These behaviors are unacceptable, and if not dealt with immediately, they can result in serious injury or death for your dog or the object of his aggression. There may be a root issue or trigger that you are not aware of, so consult a professional trainer or animal psychologist promptly if you are dealing with these truly bad and dangerous dog behaviors.

Getting to the Root of the Problem

The first step to eliminating unwanted behavior is to find out why your dog is doing it. Learning why he's exhibiting a certain behavior can make correcting or redirecting the problem much easier for you and your dog.

Instinctual – Many times, unwanted behavior stems from instinct. If this is the case, the behavior will be more challenging to stop. Consult a professional trainer for help, but also try to redirect the instinctual behavior in a positive way.

Lack of Training – Most of the unwanted behaviors on this list begin with a lack of proper training. Time spent consistently training your dog is the best way to correct these annoyances. See Chapter 10 for more training tips and how to get started.

Past Trauma – If you are dealing with aggression issues, consider any traumas in your dog's past, especially if you adopted him later in his life. These issues need to be dealt with by a trained professional, so seek help immediately.

How to Correct Your Dog

Punishment is not an effective way to correct unwanted behaviors in your dog. As discussed previously, your Boykin Spaniel will want to please you with his actions, so if he's doing something undesirable, it's because he isn't sure what is right. Correct him by showing him what you want him to do and not what you don't want him to do. Reward him for positive behavior, and he is sure to catch on quickly.

When to Call a Professional

Usually, unwanted behaviors in dogs are just annoyances and not "bad." However, even behaviors that come naturally to your dog can become dangerous if left unchecked. Digging holes in the yard is irritating, but it becomes a safety issue if your Boykin Spaniel begins digging those holes under the fence. Chewing can be upsetting when your favorite pair of sandals fall victim, but it is not inherently dangerous. On the other hand, chewing on an electrical cord can be deadly.

If your attempts to redirect the behavior have been unsuccessful, seek a professional trainer's help. They have seen these issues time and time again and will have the resources and experience to find a solution that works for both you and your dog. The longer you wait, the harder these bad habits will be to break.

CHAPTER 17

Caring for Your Senior Boykin Spaniel

Just like humans, dogs may experience a decline in health as they age into their senior years. Conditions such as arthritis, cognitive dysfunction, cataracts, hearing loss, incontinence, and an inability to regulate body temperature become typical.

According to the AKC, the lifespan of a Boykin Spaniel is 10 to 15 years. While there is no set age to determine when your dog becomes a senior, it is generally characterized by the last third of his life span. Not all dogs reach this stage at the same time, however, and many can live comfortable and happy lives for years. This chapter will discuss potential issues you may face with your aging dog and help you navigate the difficult end-of-life decisions when the time comes.

Common Old-Age Ailments

Arthritis – Osteoarthritis is a degenerative joint disease where the bones of a joint rub against each other due to the deterioration of the cartilage between them. This deterioration can cause severe pain, stiffness, and limited mobility. Osteoarthritis cannot be cured, but it can be treated with medication and supplements to slow the progression of the disease and treat symptoms.

Cataracts – Cataracts cause a dog to have blurry vision by creating an opacity in the normally clear lens. If your senior dog develops cataracts, have your vet monitor him closely for worsening symptoms. When left untreated, cataracts can sometimes lead to blindness. While this is not a death sentence for your Boykin Spaniel, it would take a major life adjustment for you and him. That said, many blind dogs live happy and healthy lives!

Cognitive Dysfunction – Senior dogs are susceptible to dementia, just like humans are. If you notice your dog forgetting something he does often or acting unusually out of his normal routine, discuss options with your vet for helping improve his quality of life. If your dog experiences these symptoms, try to ease his frustration and confusion by making

Photo Courtesy of
Jason Martin

everyday tasks simpler for him. This could mean putting his food and water in a more visible place in the house, leading him outside more often or using a puppy pad to avoid accidents, and keeping his toys and belongings easily accessible.

Just like with humans, dogs with cognitive dysfunction can benefit greatly from mental stimulation. Continue to review and practice basic commands, such as sit and stay with your senior dog or a basic game of hide-and-seek with a toy. These activities can help to slow the worsening of this condition and can help improve memory.

Hearing Loss – Hearing loss is common for old dogs. While many will lose some degree of hearing, they may not go completely deaf. Signs of hearing loss include a sudden lack of obedience, increased startle reaction, and excessive barking.

If your dog experiences hearing loss, you may need to find another form of communication. Teach your dog hand signals at the first sign of hearing loss so that if he loses his hearing completely, you can still communicate commands. It may also be helpful to keep a flashlight handy to signal for his attention.

> *Give your dog lots of love; the golden years come too soon! You will see the dog take stairs more slowly, lose footing, and jump less but snuggle just as much. As hearing or eyesight becomes less effective, other senses often heighten. Your patience, encouragement, observations and empathy go a long way to meeting their changing needs. Ensure older dogs have plenty to drink and provide ample chance to go outside to avoid bladder infections. Keep their ears clean, as ear infections can also plague older dogs of all breeds. Continue with regular vet visits as they can help identify infections or other issues that can be addressed with medications or a switch in foods. Your dog's loyalty and love will last a lifetime and echo even longer in your heart.*
>
> SHAWN MARIE DOUGHERTY
> *SOHO Edition Boykin Spaniels*

Basic Senior Dog Care

> **"**
>
> *They say Boykins are like potato chips—you can't have just one! While some people might think getting a puppy is hard on an older dog, I think, in a lot of cases, it brings life to them and keeps them young. I personally have four Boykins, and they thrive on having a pack and visibly love on each other.*
>
> AUDRA BOYKIN
> *Legacy Boykins*
>
> **"**

Care for a senior dog should be focused on keeping him comfortable and happy. Like people, senior dogs have trouble regulating their body temperature. Be sure to provide your dog with extra warmth on a cold day, and make sure he stays cool on a hot day.

Special accommodations may need to be made to make life more comfortable for your aging dog. For example, if your dog has arthritis, he may benefit from a bed made specifically to help with stiffness. If you have stairs, you may also need to consider keeping all your dog's things on the lowest level of your home so he doesn't need to climb the stairs. A step stool to help him reach his favorite spot on the couch may also be nice.

As a dog ages, energy levels usually decline along with stamina. It's important that you still give your aging dog regular, gentle exercise to keep him in shape. Obesity can be a problem in older dogs, who typically move around less, and it can exacerbate other age-related ailments such as arthritis and heart conditions. If obesity becomes a problem despite regular exercise, discuss options with your veterinarian. He or she may suggest switching to a different food or changing portion size.

Your senior dog will probably need to see the vet more in his last years. The AAHA (American Animal Hospital Association) recommends that you take your senior dog to the vet at least once every six months for a check-up. These regular vet visits can help you catch any conditions early and allow for more prompt treatment, potentially leading to a better quality of life.

Illness and Injury Prevention

> "
>
> *Your aging Boykin will still be young at heart and will still want to hunt and do all the activities it has always enjoyed. You will need to watch out for the dog and protect it from overheating and over-exertion. Keep a close eye on your Boykin in the field, and always plan ahead so that you can get it back to the truck when necessary.*
>
> PATRICIA DOWNEY
>
> *Bayhill Boykins*
>
> "

Illness and injury prevention are crucial for any aging dog. Illness and injury are both more difficult to overcome for a senior Boykin Spaniel than a young one. The best way to prevent injury and illness is to know your dog's changing limits. Adapt your Boykin Spaniel's exercise routine to meet his needs and limitations. Just remember, exercise is extremely important for an older dog, so do not stop exercising him completely.

Because your aging dog is more prone to injury, exercise should be done more slowly and with little to no impact on joints. This means no jumping, climbing, or walking at an incline for a prolonged period. Instead, try a slow, leisurely walk or a swim. If you notice your dog limping after exercise, dial it back and take it easier to avoid injury or pain.

Also, staying up to date on your dog's vaccinations and medications, including flea and tick preventatives, can go a long way in helping to keep him well in his later years. If your elderly dog does become ill, he is more likely to suffer life-threatening complications than his younger counterparts. A case of kennel cough may be no big deal for a young dog, but it could quickly lead to a dangerous case of pneumonia for a senior dog.

Ultimately, you will need to be patient with your Boykin Spaniel as he ages and remember that this is a normal life progression. Adjustments will need to be made and lifestyle changes implemented. Try to enjoy the later years with your dog and learn to slow down with him.

Photo Courtesy of
Austin Barkley

> Boykins may suffer from joint stiffness as they age. There are many supplements to help with this. Aging Boykins may require less strenuous exercise but will still need to be mentally challenged to stay happy and fit. Swimming is an excellent source of exercise for the aging dog.
>
> EDITH HINES
> *Woodland Holler Boykins*

Supplements and Nutrition

Good nutrition is still key to keeping your senior dog in his best shape, even in the later years. Quality of life is directly affected by nutrition, including supplements. Though there are supplements on the market formulated for senior dogs, always ask your vet before adding anything to your dog's diet, as there is a potential for side effects and drug interactions.

Here is a list of the most common supplements used for senior dogs.

Glucosamine and Chondroitin – Two supplements often paired together to combat osteoarthritis, glucosamine and chondroitin, have been found to be therapeutic in the treatment of canine arthritis. These compounds are found naturally in cartilage and are made by the body.

When looking for a glucosamine and chondroitin supplement, look for highly reputable brands that source all their ingredients from the United States. Imported glucosamine has been found to contain many contaminants, including lead, especially when sourced from China. Since the FDA does not regulate supplements, the only way to know if you are getting a quality product is to be vigilant and diligent in your research. Even popular pet store brands that say "made in the USA" can include ingredients sourced from China.

Omega-3 Fatty Acids – Omega-3 fatty acids like DHA and EPA have been shown to be beneficial to the brain, potentially improving cognitive function in old age, and they may even give your dog's immune system a boost. According to the AKC, "The addition of omega-3 to the diet may [also] help reduce inflammation and can promote cell membrane health."

Antioxidants – Including an extra source of antioxidants in your senior Boykin Spaniel's diet can be beneficial as well. You can do this by purchasing a supplement or by simply allowing your dog to snack on high-antioxidant fruits such as berries and apples.

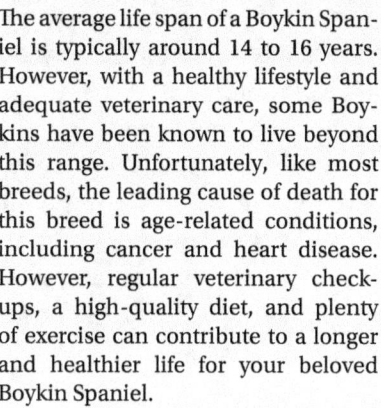

HELPFUL TIP

The average life span of a Boykin Spaniel is typically around 14 to 16 years. However, with a healthy lifestyle and adequate veterinary care, some Boykins have been known to live beyond this range. Unfortunately, like most breeds, the leading cause of death for this breed is age-related conditions, including cancer and heart disease. However, regular veterinary check-ups, a high-quality diet, and plenty of exercise can contribute to a longer and healthier life for your beloved Boykin Spaniel.

Probiotics – Probiotics help maintain healthy bacteria in the gut, the place where up to 80% of a dog's immune defenses reside. This can improve immune function and help your senior dog fight off illness and disease more efficiently.

> 66
>
> *Remember that your Boykin has earned the right to retire. Be kind and patient. Do whatever it is that makes the dog happy. Supplements for joint health can be added to the diet. Enjoy every moment with your dog and squeeze every bit of joy out of the ride. It will be over way too soon.*
>
> DAWN CRITES
> *Lily Pad Spaniels*
> 99

When It's Time to Say Goodbye

Understanding when the end is near for your Boykin Spaniel can be one of the most difficult aspects of ownership. No one wants to face saying goodbye to a loyal companion and friend, but, ultimately, it is our responsibility as owners and caretakers to be loving and selfless as a dog nears this time.

When the time comes, and your Boykin Spaniel may be experiencing more pain than happiness, it may be time to consider humanely ending his life to relieve him from the pain. This decision is never made easily and can lead to an array of emotions for the owner, including sorrow, guilt, and, oftentimes, second thoughts. These emotions are normal and will likely be there no matter how many times you are faced with a dog's end-of-life decisions.

Treat your Boykin as part of your family. The dog will give you its heart and soul all its life, and it deserves your love and affection for its whole life. Follow your vet's recommendations as the dog ages to keep it as comfortable as possible as long as possible. When it's time to let the dog go, be with it, as painful as it is. The dog has loved you its entire life, and it deserves for you to be with it at the end.

MARK LEE
Holland Ridge Boykins

How Will You Know When the Time Is Right?

Trust your instincts as a loving caretaker. You and your Boykin Spaniel have formed a bond that no one else may know the depth of; therefore, you are the most qualified to make the call.

If you have a gut feeling that your Boykin Spaniel has made a sharp decline in health and is hurting more than he is not, the time may be right to make the call. A few telltale signs that death is imminent are extreme lethargy, lack of interest in anything, loss of coordination, incontinence, and not eating or drinking.

Photo Courtesy of Kayla Mims

Only you and your dog will know when this time is. Your dog has trusted you with his life thus far, and he trusts you with it now. If you believe putting him down humanely will end his suffering, speak to your vet and discuss euthanasia.

Once you have made the decision that the time has come to humanely end your dog's suffering, know that second thoughts are normal. This decision will always be hard. Don't second guess the decision that is best for your dog just because it's hard for you. Grieving over this decision, even before it has happened, is natural and normal. Talk to a trusted therapist, friend, or family member to help you cope during this difficult time.

Once you have made the decision, and if the vet agrees death is inevitable, the process happens fairly quickly. The point is to end your dog's suffering, so there is no sense in putting it off.

The Euthanasia Process

Before you take your dog to the vet, call anyone who may want to say goodbye to him. Some even choose to host a special day with their dog, feeding him all his favorite foods and taking him to see his favorite spots one last time. If you choose to do this, make it a happy and relaxed day for your dog.

When it's time, you will have the option to be present when the vet performs the procedure. Although it may be hard for you to watch your dog die, know that it will bring your dog comfort and peace in his last moments if you are there with him, holding him and comforting him.

During the procedure, your vet will administer a solution, typically phenobarbital, intravenously. The solution is usually thick with a blue, pink, or purple tint. The vet may inject it directly into a vein or into an intravenous catheter. Once the solution is injected, it will quickly travel through your dog's body, causing him to lose consciousness within just a few seconds. Your Boykin Spaniel will feel no pain. Breathing will slow and then stop altogether. Cardiac arrest will occur and cause death within 30 seconds of the injection.

Your vet will check for signs of life and will most likely step out of the room for a few moments to give you time to say a final goodbye. Your vet and his office staff have been through this before and will understand the emotional weight of the situation. They should provide you with privacy and be a source of comfort if needed. Be sure to make payments and after-death arrangements beforehand so you don't have to deal with it while you are grieving.

Your dog's body may still move after death, so don't be alarmed if you see twitching. He may also release bodily fluids, and this is also normal. When you are ready, leave your dog and allow the vet to proceed with his remains.

Making Final Arrangements

Cremation is a common choice for pet owners facing the death of a beloved dog. It is more affordable than a cemetery plot and allows you to keep your dog close to you via his ashes if you choose to do so. If you have chosen to have your dog cremated, your vet will coordinate with a cremation service and notify you when his ashes are ready.

If you are taking your deceased dog home for burial, the vet will place your dog's remains in a container and will typically carry it out to the car for you. Depending on where you live, burying your dog at home may or may not be legal. Check local laws ahead of time.

Even if it is legal, burying your dog at home may not be the best idea. Wild animals may attempt to dig up your dog's remains, flood waters can cause his body to resurface, and even groundwater contamination is possible. If you want to have a memorial at your home, consider spreading his ashes there and placing a memorial stone instead of a burial.

A pet cemetery is another option for a final resting place for your Boykin Spaniel. This is a graveyard designated just for pets. The service is not cheap. A plot can cost around $400 to $600, and that doesn't include the cost of the casket. While it is pricey, it is a beautiful place for your dog to remain among other beloved pets.

Whichever you choose, once you leave the vet's office, be prepared to grieve your loyal and loving Boykin Spaniel. Grieving the loss of a pet is serious, and you should seek professional help if you are struggling. Just remember, the love and bond you and your dog shared is not lost. It remains in your heart and memories forever.

The soul of a beloved dog is unlike any other. The utter devotion and loyalty that dogs display is unparalleled. There is simply nothing to compare it to. Dogs love with their entire being and hold absolutely NOTHING back. They exude love through every wag of their tails, whether long or short, and through every single lick of their tongues. We definitely do not deserve such unflappable adoration and pure love.

EDITH HINES
Woodland Holler Boykins

www.ingramcontent.com/pod-product-compliance
Lightning Source LLC
Chambersburg PA
CBHW071742120626
46550CB00002B/622